ECONOMIC HISTORY

ECONOMY AND SOCIETY IN NINETEENTH CENTURY BRITAIN

THE UK

ECONOMY AND SOCIETY IN NINETEENTH CENTURY BRITAIN

RICHARD TAMES

Routledge
Taylor & Francis Group
LONDON AND NEW YORK

First published in 1972

Reprinted in 2006 by
Routledge
2 Park Square, Milton Park, Abingdon, Oxon, OX14 4RN

Routledge is an imprint of Taylor & Francis Group

Transferred to Digital Print 2010

British Library Cataloguing in Publication Data
A CIP catalogue record for this book
is available from the British Library

Economy and Society in Nineteenth Century Britain
ISBN isbn (volume)
ISBN 0-415-37841-9 (subset)
ISBN 0-415-28619-0 (set)

Routledge Library Editions: Economic History

Economy and Society in Nineteenth-Century Britain

By the same author

Documents of the Industrial Revolution
Essay Techniques in Economic History

ECONOMY AND SOCIETY IN NINETEENTH-CENTURY BRITAIN

Richard Tames

London · George Allen & Unwin Ltd
Ruskin House Museum Street

First published in 1972

ISBN 0 04 942102 6 Hardback
0 04 942103 4 Paperback

Acknowledgements

The authors and publishers wish to thank the following for permission to reprint copyright material from the works listed below:

Cambridge University Press for an extract from P. Deane and W. A. Cole, *British Economic Growth, 1688–1959*; Macmillan and Co. for an extract from D. H. Aldcroft and H. W. Richardson, *The British Economy, 1870–1939*; Macmillan and Co. and the Economic History Society for two extracts from S. B. Saul, *The Myth of the Great Depression*; Longmans and Co. for an extract from S. G. Checkland, *The Rise of Industrial Society in England, 1815–85* and for an extract from W. M. Stern, *Britain, Yesterday and Today*; Methuen and Co. for two extracts from P. Mathias, *The First Industrial Nation, 1700–1914*; Penguin Books Ltd for an extract from J. Burnett, *A History of the Cost of Living*, and extracts from E. J. Hobsbawm, *Industry and Empire*.

Diagrams 1, 7, 8, 11, 12 and 13 are taken from E. J. Hobsbawm, *Industry and Empire* and are reproduced by kind permission of Penguin Books Ltd.

Contents

Diagrams and Graphs

Chapter 1

A CENTURY OF ECONOMIC GROWTH

In 1801 the population of Great Britain was 10.6 million; by 1901 it was 37.1 million. The national product in 1801 has been valued at £138,000,000; by 1901 it was £1,948,000,000. The rise per head was from £12.9 to £52.5 and, as these figures represent constant prices, the rise in material standards is evident, even allowing for the unequal distribution of socially created wealth. As evidence of economic growth the figures speak for themselves.

All three sectors had undergone periods of rapid expansion – agriculture in the first decade and a half of the century, industry intermittently over the next sixty years, services in the last third of the century – and their relationship to one another had changed. Agriculture declined from a position of relative dominance, to one of relative unimportance, while manufacturing industry and services (transport, retailing, commerce) took its place. The change-over was marked by the fact that cycles in trade and investment, rather than the fortunes of the domestic harvest, came to determine the general level of economic activity in any one year. At the beginning of the nineteenth century, machine-based factory industry was the exception: by the end of the century it was the rule. Not only had the coal, iron and cotton industries expanded their output to unprecedented orders of magnitude, but wholly new features had appeared to transform economic life. The railway, the steamship and the electric telegraph revolutionised communications; the mass-production of steel gave industry a new raw material; electricity gave it a new source of power. The joint-stock company and the trade union emerged as new means of mobilising the forces of capital and labour. But these changes were accomplished as a result of a jerky and untidy growth process in which chance factors like war and weather combined with the underlying forces of social and technological change to complete the work of economic transformation. This chapter attempts to present a brief outline of this process.

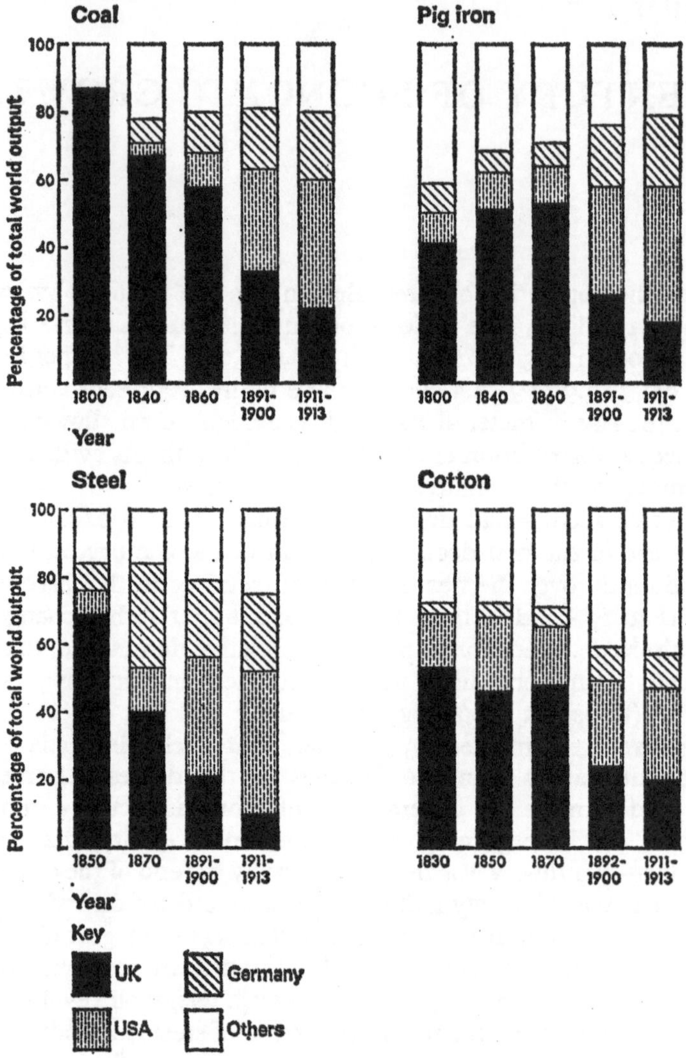

1 Britain in a Century of Growth

1793–1815. THE REVOLUTIONARY AND NAPOLEONIC WARS

. . . the country, during a war of twenty-five years, demanding exertion and an amount of expenditure unknown at any former

> period, attained to a height of political power which confounded its foes and astonished its friends . . .
>
> . . . But peace at length followed, and found Great Britain in possession of a new power in constant action, which, it may be safely stated, exceeded the labour of *one hundred millions* of the most industrious human beings, in the full strength of manhood. . . . Thus our country possessed, at the conclusion of the war, a productive power, which operated to the same effect as if her population had been actually increased fifteen- or twenty-fold: and this has been chiefly created within the preceding twenty-five years.

Thus Robert Owen, factory-owner, philanthropist and grandfather of British socialism, summarised the impact of the French wars on the British economy. There can be little doubt that he regarded it as a challenge to which Britain had responded magnificently by a great burst of capital investment in the new technology of steam. But the effects of the war were more complex: not merely a stimulus to growth, but a stimulus to growth in some directions and an obstacle to growth in others. And the problem of evaluation is complicated by the fact that the effects of the wars were compounded with deep and fundamental re-adjustments already under way – most notably the progress of industrialisation and agrarian change under the dual impact of a demographic revolution and startling improvement in the transport system. Granting that Owen was largely correct in his estimate, that the economy as a whole was vastly more productive after the wars, it is necessary to investigate the fortunes of each sector in some detail.

Agriculture – still the largest sector – employed one-third of the labour force and accounted for roughly the same proportion of the National Income. Rising population, military demands for horses and grain, and a more than average number of bad harvests combined to raise the demand for food quite dramatically. As imports in quantity were neither technically nor economically feasible, the way was open for British farmers to finance, by borrowing or from inflated profits, the introduction of new agricultural techniques which would enable them to exploit market opportunities to the full. The pace of enclosure quickened, advanced practices, such as selective breeding and four-course crop rotations, became more general, and new cheap, light, durable iron implements were widely adopted. The scale of investment in agriculture was so great that it has been suggested that it absorbed more capital than industry in this crucial period. The rate of enclosure, at nearly 53,000 acres per annum, was higher in the period 1802–15 than for any other period in British history, and it has been estimated that the acreage of potatoes increased by 60 per cent between 1795 and 1814.

Industry enjoyed mixed fortunes. Heavy industry obviously prospered with the demand for war material. Iron production, for instance, quadrupled between 1788 and 1806, and there can be little doubt that the use of Cort's process for producing wrought iron with coal spread far faster than it would otherwise have done.

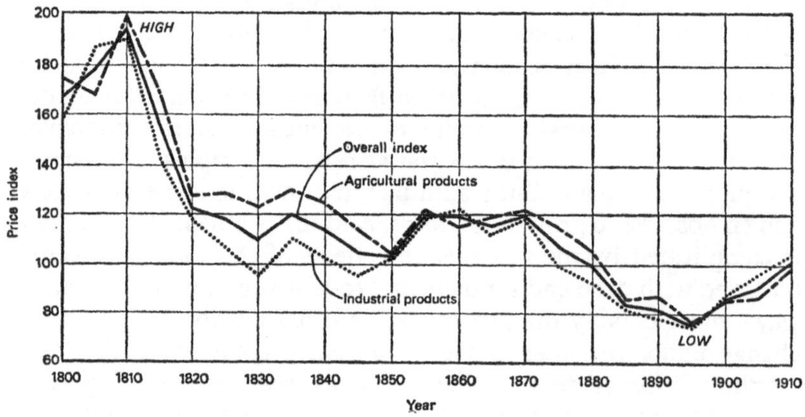

2 Rousseaux Price Indices, 1800–1913

Note: Although price data reflect in part the changing fortunes of agriculture and industry, they must be related to other indicators such as rates of growth, investment and profitability to tell the whole story.

Wool probably benefited from the demand for uniforms, but cotton, being wholly dependent on uncertain supplies of imported raw materials, grew spasmodically. Shipbuilding expanded to make good the losses incurred at the hands of the enemy, but building marked time except on government projects like barracks or docks. The more general adoption of steam-power may have been boosted by the relatively high price of fodder for horses and the scarcity of labour due to the massive recruitment of men for the armed forces.

Trade was persistently disrupted by the naval war but maintained its growth by seeking out new markets. Shut out from Europe by the 'Continental System', British traders found stable new markets in India and South America. The disasters of Napoleon's Russian campaign (1812–13) broke the façade of his authority and from then onwards British goods found their way into Europe in increasing volume.

The war cost something in the region of £1,000,000,000. Part was raised by taxation, which comprised an antiquated land-tax, a novel and much-hated income-tax, tariffs on imports and various excises on domestically produced commodities (e.g. malt). The bulk of government revenue, however, came from borrowing, with the result that the National Debt rose from around £200,000,000 to over £800,000,000 – an unprecedented development which imposed heavy burdens of debt-servicing on post-war governments and even more on the poor who paid the taxes. The other major financial feature of the period was the introduction of paper currency. A French invasion scare in 1797 produced a run on gold, and the Bank of England was obliged to make its notes non-convertible. Thereafter, paper currency became generally accepted, although the increasing volume in circulation contributed materially to war-time inflation, which boosted profits and depressed living standards.

1815–42. THE CRISIS OF CAPITALISM

The post-war period was one of disturbed and uneven growth. The pace of industrialisation quickened but against a depressing background of falling prices and severe social discontent. According to P. Deane and W. A. Cole:

> . . . the period of greatest structural change fell within the first three or four decades of the century, particularly in the two decades immediately following the Napoleonic wars. To some extent the post-war spurt was intensified by the effect of the war in distorting and retarding the pattern of growth; but probably this would have been a period of relatively rapid change even without a war to complicate the process. There was a substantial fall in the share of agriculture (amounting to perhaps 13 per cent to 14 per cent in the period 1811–41) and an equally substantial gain in the share of the mining, manufacturing and building groups of industries (*British Economic Growth 1688–1959*).

The period 1815–21 was particularly troubled. Trade, after enduring a brief re-stocking boom as goods were rushed to starved European markets, collapsed in 1818. The cessation of government orders for war material brought depression and unemployment in the iron, wool and shipbuilding industries. Agriculture was disturbed by a succession of bounteous harvests and the fear of foreign corn imports. Demobilisation released 300,000 men on to the labour market, but surplus capital, rather than seek profitable outlets by employing them, fled to the restored governments of Europe. Rapid deflation, to prepare for the resumption of cash payments (which took place in 1821), reduced the volume of money and credit, discouraging domestic investment. Falling interest rates did help the construction industry, and the consumer goods industries (like brewing and milling) picked up, but generally the period was marked by widespread social discontent. Radicals, like Orator Hunt, found large audiences ready to listen to pleas for government action and reform. The government continued to trust to political repression (e.g. Six Acts 1819) and economic fatalism.

In a sense, events justified their do-nothing policy (though *they* were in no danger of starving as a result of it). In 1822 European trade began to revive and with it industrial output and incomes. Foreign investment reached out to South America, which promised great things. The repeal of the Bubble Act (1825) produced a rash of joint-stock ventures. Their hopes were soon dashed by a general commercial crisis which engulfed South America and brought down many of the new companies. Heavy industry was depressed throughout 1826 and 1827 and there were bad harvests in 1828 and 1830. This scarcely helped the farmers, who were still producing more than the market needed, and necessitated moderate imports of grain which meant an outflow of gold, contracting credit and discouraging investment.

The atmosphere brightened in the early 1830s. Railway investment went through its first mania (1834–6) as eager speculators strove to imitate the success of the Liverpool and Manchester Railway (opened 1830). Cotton investment soared as manufacturers switched to power-weaving. Anglo-American trade doubled between 1830 and 1836, and an enlarged flow of capital across the Atlantic strengthened the economic links between the countries. Harvests were good from 1833 to 1835 and, following the reform of Parliament and the electoral system in 1832, a great number of institutional reforms were set on foot – the Factory Act (1833), abolition of slavery (1833) the New Poor Law (1834), the Municipal Reform Act (1835), the Tithe Commutation Act (1836) and civil registration (1836).

Gloom descended again after 1836 as the American market ceased to expand. Exports to America sank from £12.5 million in 1836 to £5 million in 1837. For the first time ever cotton imports fell in two successive years. Railway investment was checked and both coal and iron were plunged into an over-production crisis. The harvests of 1838 and 1839 were bad and in the latter year the country entered the deepest depression of the century. It brought down the reforming Whig administration (1841) and raised Chartist agitation to its height.

Professor S. G. Checkland has written:

> The period from the twenties to the forties is difficult to summarise. In terms of capital formation, the development of new skills, and the increase of total output, it was a time of great progress. But in terms of improvement of real wages, though many workers were gaining ground, it is highly doubtful whether the mass of men enjoyed any great material advance. Certain groups suffered heavy direct blows, the prelude to their diminution or eclipse. Prices as a whole fell continuously, except for hectic boom intervals, suggesting in a *prima facie* way that the system was not reaching its full potential output (*The Rise of Industrial Society in England, 1815–85*).

1842–73. THE GREAT VICTORIAN BOOM

The period from 1842 to 1873 was the great Victorian boom, when spasmodic growth gave way to regular and rapid growth. The basic determinants of this phase of expansion were a continuing rise in population (a world-wide, not just a British phenomenon), the rapid construction of railways, the general exploitation of steam technology by industry, and the adoption of free trade policies. Acting and re-acting upon one another, these forces of change effectively opened up a new frontier, a vacuum of demand and a new potentiality of supply, which launched industrialisation into its second phase and gave heavy industry a pivotal role in the new economy.

Recovery from the depression of 1839–42 was initiated by the second, and greatest, 'railway mania'. The European harvest crisis of 1846–7 brought it to a halt and for the last time commerce suffered the contractions induced by the 'grain in–gold out' pattern. The lag between railway promotion and railway construction, however, gave a much-needed boost at this difficult time and as a consequence Britain was saved from the revolutionary wave which engulfed Europe in 1848. The discovery of gold in Australia (1848) and California (1849) produced an atmosphere of business optimism and simultaneously provided the means to ease the problem of international payments. Exports expanded faster than industrial output, rising 130 per cent between 1842 and 1857.

The Great Exhibition (1851) demonstrated Britain's industrial supremacy to the world and it was this industrial supremacy which was the basis of her economic dominance. As Marx and Engels rather unflatteringly put it:

> The bourgeoisie, by the rapid improvement of all instruments of production, by the immensely facilitated means of communication, draws all, even the most barbarian, nations into civilisation. The cheap prices of its commodities are the heavy artillery with which it batters down all Chinese walls.... In one word, it creates a world after its own image.

The image, at least as far as Britain went, was one of prosperity. Real wages were showing the first signs of a general move upwards. Agriculture was doing well and society was stable, and the two facts were not unrelated. Attempts were being made to improve the lethal and wretched urban environment.

The Crimean War (1854–6) boosted shipping and heavy industry, but the more general availability of limited liability status (1855) led to the mushroom growth of irresponsible and ill-managed joint-stock ventures, which were swept away by the commercial crisis precipitated by the Indian Mutiny (1857). The speed of recovery was remarkable, however, and is a testimony to the underlying optimism and resilience of the mid-Victorian economy.

From 1857 to 1866 the upward trend was resumed. A new, mass-production steel industry was born, and domestic railway construction blossomed again. Steam-technology affirmed its dominance in shipbuilding. The American Civil War (1861–5) produced a 'cotton famine' in Lancashire, but brought new prosperity to India, which rose from the wreckage of the Mutiny to become temporary supplier of raw materials to one of Britain's greatest 'staple' industries. But the cessation of hostilities in America and the collapse of the railway boom in Britain brought disaster again to India and an end to the reckless speculations which had been encouraged by the discount houses of the City of London. The greatest of them, Overend, Gurney and Co., closed its doors in 1866. It was the most important financial institution after the Bank of England, and it brought down with it dozens of smaller discount houses, banks and railway companies. Widespread revelations of low business ethics and unsound managerial practices followed, and 'Black Friday' was long remembered in the City with a shudder. In retrospect, however, it might be regarded as merely a traumatic phase of 'natural selection', which left City institutions wiser, stronger and more self-restrained.

The Continental wars of 1866 (Prussia *v.* Austria) and 1870–1 (Prussia *v.* France), together with the resumption of railway construction in America, gave a terrific boost to the iron industry. Exports, at £7.50 a ton, had stood at 2,000,000 tons in 1868; by 1872 they had reached 3,300,000 and the average price had risen to £10 a ton. Coal and shipbuilding naturally shared in this expansion, and were similarly checked when German and American demand collapsed and the economy as a whole entered a new phase around 1873.

1873–96. THE GREAT DEPRESSION

The years 1873–96 are traditionally referred to by historians as the 'Great Depression'. In a recent, authoritative survey of this period, significantly entitled *The Myth of the Great Depression*, Professor S. B. Saul has argued that:

> As regards the 'Great Depression' itself, surely the major outcome of modern research has been to destroy once and for all the idea of the existence of such a period in any unified sense. The last quarter or so of the nineteenth century was a watershed for Britain as competition developed overseas and the rate of growth markedly slackened. But the process was probably under way before 1870 and most certainly continued unabated – at least in statistical terms – after 1900.

Professor Saul goes on to illustrate his point by stressing that key indicators of economic performance exhibited no uniform pattern of movement:

The terms of trade changed their movement in the middle of the period and continued in the new direction well after 1895. Low profits ruled to 1895 *and* after 1901. The great boost to real wages came in the boom to 1873 and the process was repeated again from 1896 to 1900. Real freight rates did not begin to fall until about 1880 and continued to do so almost to 1914. The downward trend in prices – traditionally the dominant feature of the 'Great Depression' may also have been under way by the mid-1860s and in several respects had ended its movement by the mid-1880s.

Professor Saul concludes, however, that:

> This is not to ignore the fact that at some time during the last quarter of the nineteenth century, Britain and several countries overseas went through unusual and worrying economic experiences which sometimes *they characterised at the time as 'a great depression'* [author's italics]. What is in question is the suggestion that this was a special feature of the years 1873–96. . . . Undoubtedly the fall of prices and the impact this had upon agriculture in particular in many parts of the world contributed to the feeling of gloom. Undoubtedly, too, it was a period of rapid change and disturbance. All this, however, is very different from picking out the years 1873–96 as having a peculiar significance either nationally or internationally. . . .

So what is there left? First, the character of this period – if indeed it can be regarded as a 'period'. It was a strange sort of depression which saw production rising unchecked (though with diminishing speed), with unemployment little higher than 'normal' (whatever that might be), and with living standards rising more swiftly than ever before. Alfred Marshall, the distinguished economist, observed that there was a depression of prices, profits and interest-rates – no other sort of depression. It is significant that he emphasised depression in what are, for the individual entrepreneur, the key indicators of economic success, and also that his observation was part of his evidence to a Royal Commission investigating the causes of what it, and the well-to-do voters and lobbyists who had clamoured for its appointment, believed *was* a depression. Their faith in the old shibboleths of *laissez-faire* was undoubtedly shaken; cartels and trade associations were formed in many industries to control prices and output as a protection for costly fixed investments. There were even mutterings about a return to tariffs. These contemporary fears, limited very largely to the owners or controllers of resources and echoed by the more articulate trade union leaders of the period (who accepted liberal economics and represented trades like shipbuilding which *did* suffer relatively high rates of unemployment), have come down to the present in the shape of the 'Myth of the Great Depression', which hangs like an albatross around the historian's neck. The inarticulate masses, who made no speeches, wrote no editorials and engaged in no learned debates, were without doubt content to enjoy the fruits of 'depression'.

Failure to examine this complex phenomenon with care, failure to define just what a particular historian regards as depressed, has led to a widespread search for 'causes'. Almost every significant economic development of the period has been summoned to do duty as a cause: transport improvements which resulted in drastic falls in freight costs; a general glut among the agricultural nations which limited their capacity to absorb exported manufactures; the absence of gold discoveries or major wars to boost optimism and investment; the erection of tariff barriers by the major industrial nations, which stifled the growth of international trade; the technological stagnation of British industry, which resulted in falling productivity; the absence of significant new inventions to precipitate a general wave of new investment. 'Results' are also legion: the trend to larger units in industry; the emergence of both socialism and imperialism; the surge in emigration; and the widespread adoption of electricity and machine-tools. So far the debate on the 'Great Depression' has generated more heat than light. Statistics, definitions and general theories abound, but confusion rather than clarity is the result so far. What the student needs to know is how and why historians disagree in their estimations of this period, and what 'causes' and 'results' they have assigned to it. A straightforward summary of the main issues of the debate and an awareness of its complexity are more useful than attempts to force the data to fit one chosen theory or to reconcile contradictory view-points into a coherent argument.

1896–1914. INDIAN SUMMER

If 1873–96 cannot be treated as a 'period', it implies that 1896–1914 cannot be either. Conventionally it is, however, and it does have distinctive features – most notably a revival of business optimism. Although the underlying deceleration of British economic growth continued, gold discoveries in the Yukon and South Africa revived business confidence. Agriculture was completing its re-adjustment to the challenge of imported foodstuffs. Heavy industry benefited from the Boer War (1899–1902) and the 'naval race' with Germany. Foreign investment revived after 1905, and reached new heights in 1910–13. It was accompanied by a torrent of emigration to Canada and Australia, possibly a reaction to the stagnation of real wages, which brought a new bitterness to labour relations. At least one-third of the population still lived in abject poverty and British industry was lagging badly behind that of her new rivals, but the pound was strong, the balance of payments healthy and the Empire safe and splendid. And yet, as E. J. Hobsbawm has written:

> . . . there was, especially in the last years before the First World War, an atmosphere of uneasiness, of disorientation, of tension, which contradicts the journalistic impression of a stable *belle époque* of ostrich-plumed ladies, country-houses and music-hall stars. . . . They were the years when wisps of violence hung in the English air, symptoms of a crisis in economy and society which the self-confident opulence of the architecture of Ritz hotels, pro-consular palaces, West-End theatres, department stores and office blocks could not quite conceal. When the war came in 1914, it was not as a catastrophe which wrecked the stable bourgeois world, as the sudden death of the breadwinner wrecked the life of respectable families in Victorian novels. It came as a respite from crisis, a diversion, perhaps even as some sort of solution . . . (*Industry and Empire*).

FURTHER READING

The following general texts are recommended for the whole period. They are all up-to-date and may be quoted with confidence. Those marked (B) have a full bibliography. All are available in paperback.

S. G. Checkland, *The Rise of Industrial Society in England, 1815–85*, (London, Longmans, 1964) is brilliant but not for beginners. (B)

P. Deane, *The First Industrial Revolution* (Cambridge University Press, 1965) covers the period 1750–1850 and has a useful sprinkling of economic theory. (B)

E. J. Hobsbawm, *Industry and Empire* (London, Weidenfeld and Nicolson, 1968) is a highly readable survey from 1750 to the present day, written from a Marxist point of view. There is an ingenious but not really usable appendix of diagrams, maps and graphs.

P. Mathias, *The First Industrial Nation, 1700–1914* (London, Methuen, 1969) is the best recent synthesis. There is a full statistical appendix. (B)

R. S. Sayers, *A History of Economic Change in England, 1880–1939* (Oxford University Press, 1965) is concise. (B)

There are a number of publishers' series devoted to economic history, notably Macmillan's Studies in Economic History, which synthesise recent works, and Methuen's Debates in Economic History, which are symposia of articles from learned journals.

The following collections of documents may prove useful:

W. H. B. Court, *British Economic History, 1870–1914* (Cambridge University Press, 1965).

G. D. H. Cole and A. W. Filson, *British Working Class Movements, 1789–1875* (London, Macmillan, 1965).

R. L. Tames, *Documents of the Industrial Revolution* (London, Hutchinson, 1971).

Chapter 2

POPULATION – ITS GROWTH, IMPACT AND MOVEMENT

THE ORIGINS OF POPULATION GROWTH

Just why population began to expand rapidly around the mid-eighteenth century is a matter of considerable dispute among demographers. Two considerable problems of evidence bedevil the issue:

1. There was no official census until 1801, and this was almost certainly inaccurate as people feared the results would be used for the purposes of taxation or conscription. The census of 1841 (which can be checked against the civil registrations of births, deaths and marriages beginning in 1836) was the first to approach modern standards of accuracy.

2. Parish registers, kept by clergy of the Church of England (the major source of evidence for pre-census population history), were particularly inaccurate in this period because of the shortcomings of the Established Church and the rise of Methodism. The result may be an under-recording of births and deaths by as much as 25 per cent in some areas.

The main outlines of growth are not, however, in dispute. After a period of unusual stagnation from 1700 to 1740, population resumed its normal upward trend (averaging 4 per cent to 7 per cent per decade in the period 1740–80) and then accelerated to over 10 per cent per decade thereafter until 1911. The decade of most rapid growth was 1811–21, when it reached 17 per cent per decade: the second greatest was the decade 1871–81 (14 per cent). The greatest addition of absolute numbers, over 4 million, did not occur till 1901–11. Thereafter the *rate* of increase declined dramatically. Population, having doubled between 1780 and 1840, and doubled again between then and the end of the century, rose by only about 50 per cent in the next sixty years.

The *causes* of this population expansion are the chief occasion of learned debate:

1. Medical factors have now been almost totally discounted. It is very doubtful whether an increased number of hospitals and better surgical techniques did save lives, and anyway the number who could afford the unpredictable medical care available in the eighteenth century were too few to be of any demographic significance. It is possible that a crude 'scratch and dab' form of inoculation helped to eliminate the killer scourge, smallpox, and also that some change in climate or ecological equilibrium brought

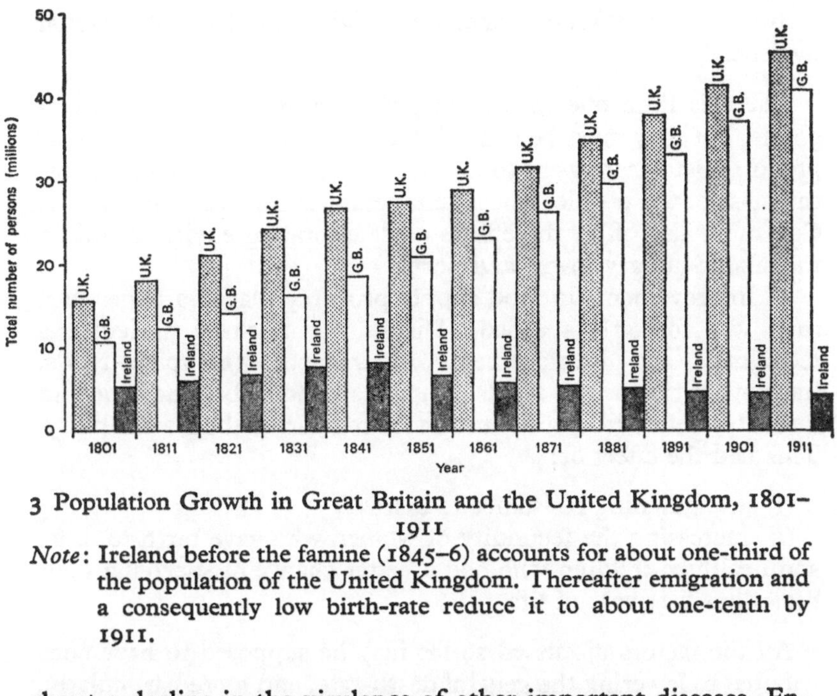

3 Population Growth in Great Britain and the United Kingdom, 1801–1911

Note: Ireland before the famine (1845–6) accounts for about one-third of the population of the United Kingdom. Thereafter emigration and a consequently low birth-rate reduce it to about one-tenth by 1911.

about a decline in the virulence of other important diseases. Enclosure and drainage of fenland may certainly have wiped out the breeding-grounds of 'ague' (malaria).

Not until the 1870s could a patient be sure of dying of the disease he was suffering from when he entered hospital. About the same time, anaesthetics and antiseptics were also rendering surgery less lethal. Only in the twentieth century has medicine (chiefly curative, but nowadays increasingly preventive) helped to prolong life, and that mainly of the elderly, who are unlikely to have more children and thus produce a 'multiplier' effect.

2. Improvements in the physical and social environment have long been a favoured explanation:

(i) more bricks and slate for cleaner, warmer housing with fewer pests;
(ii) more iron and pottery pipes for fresh water supplies and drainage;
(iii) more cheap cotton cloth for shirts, sheets and underwear which could be washed more easily than wool, leather or linen;
(iv) more cheap soap to encourage higher standards of personal hygiene.

There is little one can do to give substance to these general points, but they must be conditioned by the realisation that a disproportionate share went to the better off, and not the rural poor, the mass of the people, whose numbers increased so dramatically. One must also offset the effects of deteriorating environments in the labour-hungry towns and ports.

3. Improvements in food supply probably played a larger part than was formerly realised. Thanks to improved agricultural techniques and improvements in transport (turnpike roads, 'improved' rivers and canals), supplies of food became larger in quantity, better in quality and more regular in their availability. This had the effect of:

(i) strengthening resistance to disease;
(ii) increasing the fecundity of women who gave birth to more and healthier children who had a better chance of surviving their hazardous first year of life.

All the factors discussed so far may be supposed to have contributed to lowering the general death-rate, and more particularly, the infant mortality rate (which, because of the 'multiplier effect' of saving infants who will in turn have children, in effect raises the birth-rate). It may well be that the birth-rate also played a significant part in the 'population explosion' of the eighteenth century. The two significant factors here are:

1. The decline of 'living-in' (labourers residing with the farmer as one of the family) as an indirect consequence of the disappearance of the small farmer. This made it more essential for a labourer to marry and have a wife as a housekeeper.

2. Expanding employment opportunities as a direct consequence of economic growth. Contemporaries certainly believed this. Arthur Young, for instance, remarked that 'employment is the soul of population'.

Both these factors may have accounted for the lowering of the average age of marriage – from 27 at the beginning of the eighteenth century to 20 (in towns) and 23–24 in rural areas by the end. Earlier marriages tended to result in larger families, which were encouraged by the Speenhamland system of poor relief (which from 1795 to 1834 gave a 'dole' which varied according to the family size and the price of bread) and the ability of both factory and domestic production to find employment for children. Large families were, moreover, a poor man's form of social security. In his old age he would find food and shelter in the house of one of his children, rather than face the bleakness of the workhouse.

POPULATION IN THE NINETEENTH CENTURY

The rapid growth which began around 1740 was sustained in the nineteenth century. Death-rates, which had fallen in the late eighteenth and early nineteenth centuries, stabilised at around 22 per 1,000 between 1820 and 1870 – a development chiefly attributable to the appalling living conditions in industrial towns at that time. By the 1870s the public health campaign (which had been initiated in the 1840s to provide towns with drainage and pure water supplies) began to pay off and the general death-rate fell from 22.3 per thousand in 1871 to 13.8 per thousand in 1911 – a drop of about 40 per cent. Other contributory factors were the rising living standards (more food and clean clothes) and improved urban environments (better housing, public baths and wash-houses).

The birth-rate, which had remained fairly high throughout the century (*c.* 35 per 1,000) began to decline during the 1880s. The main causes were:

1. Children were becoming an economic burden rather than an asset, as the Factory Acts limited employment opportunities and the Elementary Education Act (1870) required their attendance at school.

2. Real incomes were rising and, for the first time, people were faced with the possibility of a sustained improvement in their way

of life. Increasingly they saw a clear choice between more children and a better life (for the children they already had, as well as for themselves) and tended to favour the latter.

3. Large numbers of young men were emigrating and this lowered the marriage-rate.

4. Birth control devices (mostly imported from Germany) were becoming cheaper and more generally obtainable. However, their mere availability does not explain why people chose to use them; this depended on factors 1 and 2. One must also remember that such 'luxuries' were beyond the reach of many of the poor (and ambitious), who simply abstained from cohabiting.

The result was a decrease in family-size, from 5 to 6 children in the 1860s to 2 to 3 in the 1920s. This tendency started among the middle classes and permeated slowly downwards through the social pyramid. (Middle-class couples may actually have suffered an 'incomes squeeze' during the price, rent and profit slump of the Great Depression of 1873–96 and therefore have limited their family-size to eke out resources on education and status symbols.)

One important statistic changed scarcely at all – the infant mortality rate. Though fluctuating year by year from 100 to 180 per thousand, it averaged about 135 per thousand in the 1890s as it had in the worst decade, the 1840s. The explanation lies in the vulnerability of infants to infectious disease in towns. Between 1901 and 1921 the rate fell dramatically, by 50 per cent approximately. This was due to:

1. The Certification of Midwives (1902).
2. The long-term effects of rising living standards (i.e. mothers were having healthier babies).
3. The decline in birth-rate and family-size which improved the mother's health and ability to cope with young children adequately.
4. The beginning of health-visiting services.

THE EFFECTS OF POPULATION GROWTH

The expansion of population and the progess of industrialisation were inextricably intertwined.

1. A rising labour force was provided to facilitate the introduction of intensive agriculture, as well as to mine coal and work in factories. Infant industries were able to draw on young, mobile

labour with no vested interest in obsolete skills and without having to offer high wages to lure it from other employments.

2. A growing market for the necessities of life (food, clothes, shelter and household goods) was provided, encouraging entrepreneurs to experiment with new techniques to enable them to produce more, faster and cheaper. This steadily expanding domestic market exerted a valuable cushioning effect whenever volatile export markets underwent a temporary recession.

It must be emphasised that population growth did not, of itself, lead to industrial progress. It had this effect because it took place in the context of an economy which was already dynamic, with abundant resources, a new technology of steam-power and machinery and a vigorous class of businessmen to exploit them. Where these were lacking – as in Ireland (or many underdeveloped countries today) – population growth simply led to mass poverty on an unprecedented scale.

A number of informed observers believed that this fate would overwhelm England in the nineteenth century. The most influential of these was the Reverend T. R. Malthus, whose *Essay on the Principle of Population as it Affects the Future Improvement of Society* was published in 1798. He argued that population always tended to increase in a geometrical progression (2, 4, 8, 16, 32) whereas food supply only increased in an arithmetical progression (2, 4, 6, 8). The former would, therefore, tend always to outrun the latter, producing wide-spread misery and eventually mass famines.

Malthus did not foresee the amazing rise in the productivity of British agriculture during the nineteenth century, nor the ability of the country to import food from the virgin soils of the New World. But his gloomy predictions carried great weight with his contemporaries, and he must take a great share of the responsibility for the harshness of Victorian attitudes towards the poor. Since any easing of their condition would encourage them to breed and multiply both the course of their poverty and the numbers who must endure, it was necessary to treat them harshly for their own, and society's, benefit.

EXTERNAL MIGRATION

During the ninteteenth century, Britain decanted her population into the empty spaces of a fast-shrinking world. The chronology of this exodus is fairly clear, despite the fact that figures for the first half of the century make it difficult to allow for those who subsequently returned.

There was no substantial outflow until 1815, but from then until the 1840s, the numbers ran into tens of thousands each year, varying widely, but touching 100,000 or more only in exceptional years like 1832 or the early 1840s. Some hundreds of these emigrants were skilled artisans, taking industrial know-how to Belgium, France, Germany or Russia. Laws against their migration were repealed in 1825, and, though numerically small, their strategic value was great. They were a loss of talent to Britain (though they might one day give export orders for, say, textile machinery) and an asset to the country which received them. Most of those who went, however, had no skill, but much initiative, and their departure relieved the critical pressure on domestic resources, particularly food and jobs.

The Irish famine of 1845–6 led to the emigration of 1,500,000 Irish in the succeeding decade. They accounted for four-fifths of all emigrants in this period, and most of them went to the U.S.A. (though often via Liverpool, Glasgow or London where they raised their fare for the crossing). The discovery of gold in Australia (1848) encouraged emigration in that direction, though a steady stream of undesirables had accepted pressing government invitations to Botany Bay for over half a century.

Railway construction in the 1850s and 1860s took many navvies to Europe and further afield, but the next great burst of movement came in the 1870s and 1880s – agricultural labourers left the land by the hundred thousand, determined to find land of their own elsewhere. Miners from dying areas like Cornwall and Derbyshire also made up a fair number, while famine and the hounding of crofters in the Highlands added more. In the 1890s fewer left, but in the decade before the Great War, a renewed burst of foreign investment led to the greatest ever outflow – 700,000 a year in the period 1910–13, two-thirds going to the Empire, particularly Canada.

Why did they go? A combination of desperate conditions at home and promising ones abroad. And it must be remembered that for the agricultural worker, the transition from the Chilterns to the Prairie was probably less difficult to contemplate or come to terms with, than the confinement and unfamiliarity of factory work would have been. William Cobbett put the position well when he wrote:

> The way to New York is now as well known and as little expensive as from old York to London. First the Sussex parishes sent their paupers; they invited over others that were not paupers; they invited over people of some property; then of greater property; now substantial farmers are going; men of considerable fortune will follow. It is the letters written across the Atlantic that do the business. . . . The United States form another England without its unbearable taxes, its insolent game laws, its intolerable dead-weight and its treadmills.

Some of the emigrants were assisted by charitable bodies, such as the Poor Law authorities and trade unions. Others went with the assistance of colonial governments. Most financed and organised their own departure, a process which was facilitated by the following factors:

1. Britain's large shipping fleet, which could provide cheap passages (£3.50 to cross the Atlantic), in admittedly appalling conditions.
2. English was the language of the U.S.A. and the Empire. Their legal systems, cultural life and climate were all broadly similar to those of England.
3. Ever-improving postal services enabled would-be emigrants to learn about opportunities and keep in touch with the more adventurous (note Cobbett's observation above). Remittances from successful emigrants often paid the fares of relatives and friends. The *Illustrated London News* observed of the Irish emigrants in 1849 that 'the great bulk appear to be people of the most destitute class, who go to join their friends and relatives, previously established in America'.

Because the majority of emigrants were young men aged 18–40, the effects of this large-scale emigration were far-reaching. The main results of their departure were:

1. The birth-rate fell (from the 1880s) and a surplus of females was left to swell the ranks of the army of domestic servants.
2. The bargaining position of labour in Britain improved, but, in occupations where strength counted, its productivity may have declined as the average age of workers rose. Attitudes of opposition to technical and organisational change may have hardened through the same process.
3. An overseas market with a preference for British goods was

constantly refreshed. This enabled British manufacturers to build up trade to the Empire, when Europe and the U.S.A. began to put up tariff walls in the 1870s and 1880s.

4. Emigration may well have acted as a social and political safety-valve, draining off would-be revolutionaries and much other inflammable material, particularly in the 'Hungry Forties'.

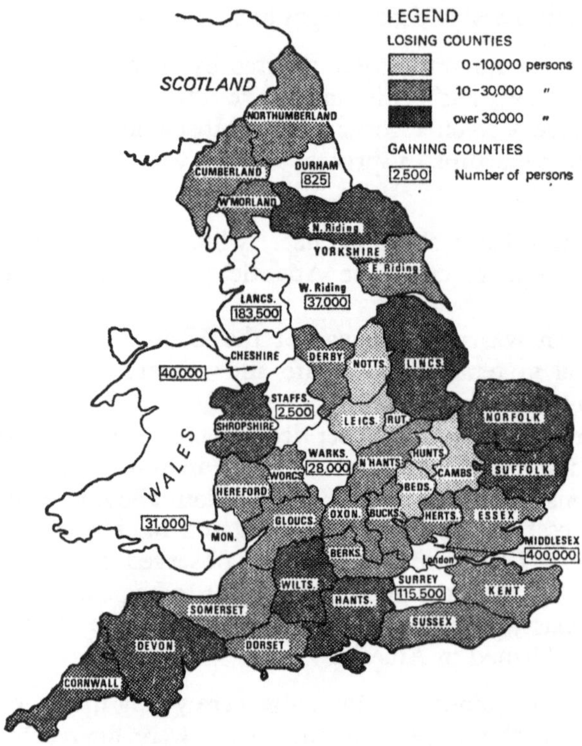

4 Internal Migration in England, 1801–31

INTERNAL MIGRATION

Most internal migration involved very short distances, usually from five to twenty-five miles. The cumulative effect of overlapping waves of migration was, however, to move the centre of gravity of population north and west, towards the coal-fields and the Atlantic ports.

It was mostly the young who went in search of employment. Married men were restrained by families, social ties and debts, as well as a tied cottage, rights of poor relief, etc. In the absence of labour exchanges and literacy, ignorance of opportunities and fear of the unknown, strange food and unfamiliar customs, were also retarding factors. Nonetheless movement was very substantial. In 1851 of the 6.5 million people who lived in London and the seventy greatest towns of the British Isles, 3 million were immigrants.

That acute journalist, Henry Mayhew, noted how large numbers lived permanently on the move.

> The nomadic races of England are of many distinct kinds – from the habitual vagrant – half-beggar, half-thief, . . . to the mechanic on tramp, obtaining his bed and supper from the trade societies in the different towns, on his way to seek work. Between these two extremes there are several mediate varieties – consisting of pedlars, showmen and harvestmen, and all that large class who live by either selling, showing, or doing something through the country. . . . Besides these, there are the urban and suburban wanderers . . . the pick-pockets – the beggars – the prostitutes – the street-sellers – the street-performers – the coachmen – the watermen – the sailors and suchlike.

He could have added 'the navvies', and it is important to remember that only a small fraction were going to find work in one of the new factories – the young labourer was far more likely to end up in the mines, the docks or the building-sites. The unsuccessful would drift into casual labour, transport or petty crime, ultimately merging with the riff-raff. Young women (who outnumbered men as migrants) found work in domestic service, the clothing trades or 'sweated' industry.

Railways promoted the mobility of labour considerably; not simply by making travel faster and cheaper, but by breaking down rural isolation and accustoming men to the idea of travel itself.

Many of the migrants were Scots or Welsh, but none were so numerous as the Irish, whose physical strength and willingness to take very low wages earned them the approbation of English employers and the hatred of English workers. They specialised in 'the most irksome and disagreeable kinds of coarse labour'. According to the *Report of the State of the Irish Poor in Great Britain* (1836):

> The Irish emigration into Britain is an example of a less civilised population spreading themselves, as a kind of substratum, beneath a more civilised community: and without excelling in any branch of industry, obtaining possession of all the lowest departments of manual labour.

Ireland had no work for its expanding numbers; seasonal employment in England had been customary for generations; the deck fare to Liverpool was *4d.* – scarcely surprising therefore that by mid-century there were 500,000 Irish in England and Wales. 100,000 were in London; they formed one-tenth of the population of Manchester and one-sixth of that of Liverpool. Scotland, with a much smaller population than that of England, had absorbed no less than 250,000 Irish, mostly in and around Glasgow, the port of reception and one of the worst cities in Europe. The problems which migration on this scale posed for urban environments will be considered in the next chapter.

FURTHER READING

The literature on demographic history is vast, and much of it is to be found only in the pages of learned journals like the *Economic History Review* or *Population Studies.*

M. W. Flinn, *British Population Growth, 1700–1850* (London, Macmillan, 1970), in Macmillan's Studies in Economic History series, provides a convenient summary and synthesis of the current debate for the novice.

M. Drake (ed.), *Population in Industrialisation* (London, Methuen, 1969), in Methuen's Debates in Economic History series, brings together half a dozen of the most important articles and has a useful introduction.

D. V. Glass and D. E. C. Eversley (eds), *Population in History* (London, Edward Arnold, 1965) contains twenty to thirty contributions from leading scholars, and deals with theoretical and comparative aspects of demographic history, as well as the British experience (Chapters 2, 4, 7, 9, 10, 15 and 17 are particularly relevant).

E. L. Jones and G. E. Mingay, *Land, Labour and Population in the Industrial Revolution* (London, Edward Arnold, 1967) contains articles on population by J. T. Krause and P. E. Razzell.

E. A. Wrigley (ed.), *An Introduction to English Historical Demography* (London, Weidenfeld and Nicolson, 1966) deals with problems of methodology.

A. Redford, *Labour Migration in England, 1800–50* (Manchester University Press, 1926: 2nd edition 1964 revised by W. H. Chaloner) is the standard work on the internal movement of population.

J. Saville, *Rural Depopulation in England and Wales* (London, Routledge, 1957) is also useful.

G. S. R. Kitson Clark, *An Expanding Society: Britain 1830–1900* (Cambridge University Press, 1967) deals with the wider aspects of emigration.

O. MacDonagh, *A Pattern of Government Growth, 1800–60* (London, MacGibbon, 1961) deals with the Passenger Acts and their enforcement.

Chapter 3

URBANISATION AND THE HOUSING PROBLEM

THE NATURE OF THE PROBLEM

The early nineteenth century was a great age of construction – but not of house-building. The building industry (which was the third greatest employer of labour in 1851) concentrated its efforts on meeting the profitable demand for factories, warehouses, docks, public buildings and railways, as industrialisation gathered pace. As Professor S. G. Checkland has remarked, the workers got what was left over, in terms of land, materials, labour and design.

The rapid growth of urban populations (Liverpool grew by 46 per cent and Manchester by 40 per cent in the single decade 1821–31) created an unprecedented need for urban housing, but this need was not, in the terms of the economist, an 'effective demand', that is a will to purchase, backed up by money. Working men and women made food, and strong drink, the first call on their family incomes. They tended to rent the cheapest accommodation, so that it could be kept on in times of slump and unemployment. Disposable incomes were too liable to wide fluctuations (due to depression, sickness, accident or a bad harvest) for them to be able to set aside a surplus which would eventually enable them to transfer to better housing. Besides, better housing was scarce, and would have been on the edges of industrial settlement, and nearly all workers had to live within walking distance of their employment. Given the rents that they were able and willing to pay, house-building, from the point of view of the builder, calculating his net return on capital outlay, was far less attractive than building for the big buyers in the market for construction services – the industrialist, the merchant and the railway company.

There were also a number of structural bottlenecks on the supply side of the building industry:

1. It did not undergo an industrial revolution in its techniques, but remained a high-cost craft industry with strong unions capable of enforcing apprenticeship regulations to restrict entry to the craft and keep up the level of wages. As economies of scale in production are less open to the manufacturer than they are in other industries, a house remained an expensive product.

2. Urban land was at a premium, and industry and the railways had first call on favourable locations, because they could pay for them. The price of materials was raised by excise charges on timber, glass and bricks until the 1840s.

3. It was an industry in which small firms, employing a dozen to fifty men, were typical. Thomas Cubitt's 1,000-man enterprise was quite exceptional and rested on his skills of organisation and his ability to maintain a steady flow of contracts for barracks, institutions and the nineteenth-century equivalent of 'exclusive executive developments'. The small builders worked on extended credit to provide their circulating capital and were the first to go under when a hint of recession obliged them to meet the calls of apprehensive creditors.

THE SOLUTION

Population continued to rise inexorably, and towns, in particular, grew in response to the demand of urban industry for labour. By mid-century the representative Englishman was a townsman and his housing problem had been dealt with by a combination of the following expedients:

1. Overcrowding of houses – by forcing as many as possible on to available acreage as 'back-to-backs' or multi-storey tenements, or by squeezing them into the gaps left between gas-works and goods yards.

2. 'Jerry-building' – skimping on labour and especially on materials, by making rooms without window-spaces, or by building them less than six feet high and by leaving out fittings such as window-frames, doors or water pipes (which were likely to be burnt or sold by destructive tenants who frequently defied all attempts to make them pay rent).

3. Overcrowding of persons – the simplest expedient of all. As the supply of houses could not keep up with the need for them, more people had to be content with less space. In 1847 in one street

in St Giles, London, nearly 1,100 persons were found to be living in 27 houses.

4. Large numbers of people appear to have had no permanent home, perhaps 50,000 in London at mid-century, including a high proportion of orphans, and casual workers. They either slept rough under railway arches or braved the hazards of a common lodging-house for a penny a night.

THE STATE OF THE TOWNS

Urbanisation, like industrialisation, was an unplanned process. Towns mushroomed and as no one was responsible for providing amenities, no one did:

1. The somnolent Church of England was too sluggish to alter its parish boundaries or its traditional hierarchical arrangements fast enough to cope with the spiritual challenge of a new change. In the towns, its traditional functions were eventually taken over by the dissenting chapels which sprang up in large numbers to crusade on behalf of literacy, temperance and self-help, as well as the Lord. In the second half of the century numerous church 'missions' and the newly-founded 'Salvation Army' conducted a renewed assault on filth, vice and ignorance.

2. Paving and lighting were inadequate, except in those better-off quarters of the older towns, where Improvement Commissioners had been active – sporadically and at cross-purposes with each other – since the 1780s. The Municipal Reform Act (1835) provided new towns with a framework of local authority to cope with the provision of such elementary urban facilities.

3. Effective drainage and water supply, which were essential for healthy and civilised living, were unavailable in most towns, as Edwin Chadwick's famous *Report on the Sanitary Condition of the Labouring Population* (1842) revealed. Consider, for instance, this description of conditions in Stockton:

> Shepherd's Buildings consist of two rows of houses [forty-four in all, each of two rooms, with twenty-two cellars used as separate dwellings] with a street seven yards wide between them. . . . There are no yards or out-conveniences: the privies are in the centre of each row, about a yard wide: over them there is part of a sleeping-room . . . in the centre [of the street] is the common gutter, or more properly sink, into which all sorts of refuse

are thrown: it is a foot in depth. Thus there is always a quantity of putrefying matter contaminating the air.

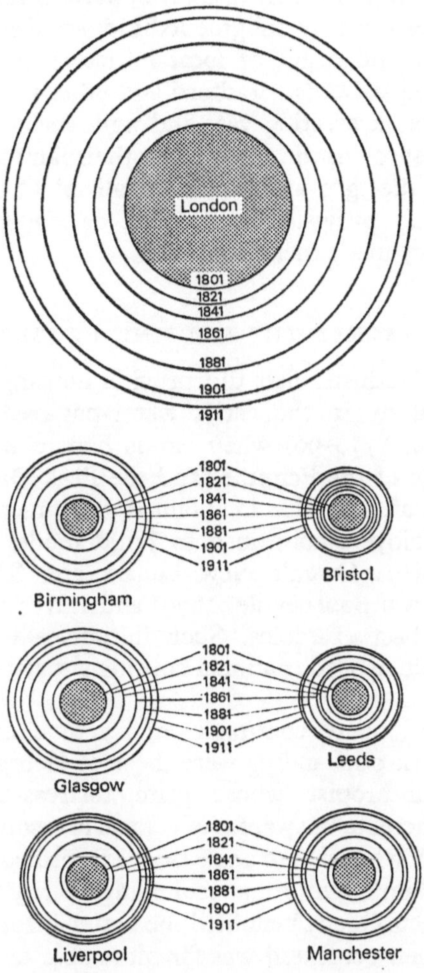

5 The Growth of Large Towns
Town populations which exceeded 30,000 in 1801 and their subsequent changes.

In the 1850s, 1860s and 1870s the work was done, thanks to the prodding of bands of doctors and health inspectors and despite the opposition of vested property interests and ratepayers who demanded 'cheap government'. The fall in the general death-rate in the 1870s showed that these measures were beginning to take effect.

4. Parks, libraries, assembly halls, etc., were included in some of the model estates built by enlightened industrialists, but in most towns they were the result of local initiative or charitable bequests. In the 1840s Leeds, Bradford and other textile towns vied with one another in erecting vast and ugly shrines to civic self-importance. Most towns did not acquire their fair share of cultural amenities until the 'gas and water socialism' of the 1880s and 1890s made their provision as feasible as rising standards of living and literacy made them desirable.

ATTEMPTS TO TACKLE THE HOUSING PROBLEM

1. A number of industrialists did provide housing for their employees, particularly in the early, water-powered phase of industrialisation (*c*. 1770–90) when hands had to be lured to the outlying districts of the Pennines and the Peak District. Isolated mining villages of necessity maintained the practice, and some enlightened employers continued to build model estates in the tradition of Robert Owen's New Lanark and Sir Titus Salt's Saltaire. Cadbury's Bourneville (1879) and Lever's Port Sunlight (1888) are the best examples. Such initiatives were rare, and, from the perspective of the national housing situation, of negligible importance.

2. There were many charitable efforts to eliminate housing horrors. The most outstanding were those of George Peabody, an American philanthropist whose grim fortress-like blocks of housing still punctuate busy areas of central and southern London, and Octavia Hill, who tried to show that refurbished housing could be let at an economic rent, thus reconciling charity with economy. Charitable projects chiefly benefited the better-off artisan, who was able to afford their rents and was far more able to make arrangements for himself than the submerged mass whose conditions were really desperate. Charity housing benefited only a few, and a select few at that, and in a sense it may have delayed solution of the housing problem by vigorous public action by deluding those who wished to be deluded that the problem was already being adequately dealt with.

3. Action by public authorities was chiefly inspired by the

public health crusade. Many of the new municipalities were swift to pass bye-laws regulating building, and central government helped with such measures as the Torrens Act (1869) which permitted demolition of individual houses and the Cross Act (1875) which did the same for larger insanitary areas. But these acts were only permissive and did not *oblige* Local Authorities to take action, though the great Public Health Act of 1875 did lay down minimum standards for height of rooms, number of windows, etc., and recodified much of the legislation previously scattered through the statute book.

Joseph Chamberlain's 'Corporation Street' scheme in Birmingham halved the local death-rate in five years, showing what could be achieved by municipal energy. But Victorian England, although willing to countenance negative regulation, was still too wedded to *laissez-faire* to give serious consideration to policies involving millions of pounds of public money, which would give something for nothing and encroach on a field of activity regarded as sacred to private enterprise.

CONCLUSION

Public awareness of the housing problem was re-awakened in the 1880s by the surveys of Booth, the pamphlets of the Reverend Mearns (*The Bitter Cry of Outcast London*) and the report of the Royal Commission on the *Housing of the Working Classes* (1884–5). This authoritative body, which contained such eminent persons as the Prince of Wales and Cardinal Manning, conducted a thorough investigation into the problem but shrank from the logic of its findings, to recommend public expenditure. It did, however, give birth to the Housing Act (1890) which started off the process of clearing the backlog of slums and laid the foundations for future policy, just as the Town and Country Planning Act (1909) familiarised authorities with the elements of environmental design. The slow pace of improvement can be judged from the fact that in 1914 more than 10 per cent of the population was still overcrowded by the low standards then considered acceptable. In such cities as Newcastle upon Tyne and Sunderland, and the East End of London, the proportion was as high as one-third, in Glasgow it was nearly one-half; while in Glamorgan, Durham and Staffordshire many industrial and mining villages remained which still had no proper drainage. Post-war Britain is still attempting to solve 'the housing problem of the nineteenth century'. It remains a cause for contemporary concern rather than a mere 'topic' for the text-books.

FURTHER READING

F. Engels, *The Condition of the Working Class in England in 1844* (London, George Allen and Unwin, 1968) and H. Mayhew, *London Labour and the London Poor* (London, Dover Publications, 1969) give contemporary descriptions of housing conditions.

W. H. B. Court, *British Economic History, 1870–1914* (Cambridge University Press, 1965) and E. Royston Pike, *Human Documents of the Industrial Revolution in Britain* (London, George Allen and Unwin, 1967) include descriptive material.

S. G. Checkland, *The Rise of Industrial Society in England, 1815–85* (London, Longmans, 1964) contains a valuable discussion of the housing problem.

E. M. Carus-Wilson (ed), *Essays in Economic History*, vol. 3 (London, Edward Arnold, 1962) includes a very useful article by T. S. Ashton, 'Some Statistics of the Industrial Revolution'.

W. Ashworth, *The Genesis of Modern British Town Planning* (London, Routledge, 1954) is the only readily available treatment in depth, although Lewis Mumford, *The City in History* (Harmondsworth, Penguin, 1966) is full of insight – and illustrations.

Chapter 4

INDUSTRY

THE PACE OF PROGRESS

The process of industrialisation changed the basic characteristics of manufacturing industry, albeit more slowly than historians once believed:

1. There was an increase in the ratio of capital to labour, as buildings and machinery – which offered higher productivity and higher profits – came to play a more significant role in manufacture and to enter the forefront of the cost-conscious manufacturer's calculations, involving him more deeply and directly in the problems of capital accumulation and investment. In capital goods industries, like shipbuilding or ironmaking, the amount of fixed capital involved, which had always been relatively high, now became higher. In consumer goods industries, such as cotton textiles, pottery and brewing, it assumed a new importance.

2. The entrepreneur, the controller of resources (raw materials, labour and capital) came to assume a more dominant role, determining the techniques of production as well as marketing the finished product. The transition of putting-out clothier or 'bagman' into 'cotton-master' typifies this metamorphosis by which the craftsman, losing control over the mode of manufacture, lost control over his own economic destiny.

3. Technology came to play a more significant role as entrepreneurs became aware of how it could enlarge the productive potential and maximise the profits on which they depended for the capital to finance further investment and growth.

By 1851 the process of industrial transformation was well under way, but by no means complete. Agriculture, domestic service and the building industry were still the greatest employers of labour. Cotton, the classic 'modern' industry, had changed over to large-plant production, but the rest of the textile industries had by no means been fully mechanised. Tailoring, shoe-making and furniture-making were still organised on small workshop lines or on the urban-garret version of the old putting-out system of cottage manufacture. With the dramatic expansion of textiles and iron and the birth and growth of engineering, the structure of the industrial sector had changed, but at the same time the 'unrevolutionised' industries had also expanded their output simply by enlarging their operations along traditional lines. The two halves of the industrial sector were interacting in their joint response to new market opportunities, but not in terms of their technology or forms of organisation.

In the second half of the nineteenth century the Industrial Revolution achieved a new maturity:

1. The heavy industry sector, the coal, iron, engineering, shipbuilding complex, came to achieve the commanding position which textiles had held at mid-century. Railway construction, at home and abroad, had provided the stimulus which steam-shipbuilding and the trend to mass-production in manufacture sustained. The 'arms race', engendered by the international tensions of the quarter century before 1914, helped to maintain this momentum.

2. An increasing proportion of manufacturing enterprises switched over to the factory mode of production. The rising real incomes of the period after 1870 induced this transition particularly in consumer goods industries (e.g. foodstuffs, like jam and biscuits, and clothing, like men's suits and boots).

3. 'Mass-production' techniques entered a new stage of sophistication. Whitworth, the prophet of standardisation, who appropriately gave his name to a standard scale, popularised the idea of uniform sizes for nuts, screws and bolts and interchangeable machine components. Continuous flow-production was further assisted by the more general adoption of devices like the endless belt, bucket-conveyor and overhead travelling crane. The increasing use of machine tools and automatic machinery made the worker into a machine supervisor and gave birth to products proudly advertised as 'untouched by hand'.

4. Science began to play a much larger part in industry:

(i) It created new products (like aniline dyes, 1856) and new processes (like the Gilchrist-Thomas 'basic' steel-making process, 1879) and utilised new raw materials (rubber, oil and manganese) and old waste-products (coal tar and scrap steel) – whose new utility led to their re-christening as by-products.

(ii) A more 'scientific', or at least rational, attitude to industrial problems emerged. 'Work study' analysed the movements of manual workers and the implications of such factors as heating, lighting, ventilation and plant layout. Chains of responsibility were established and new specialists – production engineers, cost accountants, personnel managers – emerged. The improvement of industrial techniques ceased to be the result of the flair and genius of a single personality, and became the everyday business of organised teams.

The most alarming feature of these developments was that they went much further in the U.S.A. and Germany than in Great Britain. It was in America that 'scientific management' first emerged through the efforts of F. W. Taylor. It was in America that 'machine-made machines' were first produced on a large scale – the Colt revolver (1835), the typewriter (1843), the Yale lock (1855), the Singer sewing-machine (1850) – all tributes to 'Yankee' ingenuity. And by 1914 the American worker had about five times as much capital at his disposal as his British counterpart. Little wonder that his relative output was so much higher.

THE STAPLE INDUSTRIES

The most remarkable thing about the staple industries was that they remained staple for so long. Dominating the industrial sector at the end of the Napoleonic wars, cotton, coal, iron and steel and engineering still accounted for nearly half the value added by manufacture, according to the 1907 census of production. In terms of numbers employed and capital invested they towered over the 'growth' industries of the twentieth century – vehicles, chemicals and electrical goods. Unfortunately the robust machinery and primitive techniques which had carried them so triumphantly through the first phase of industrialisation, hung around the staple industries like much-loved millstones, becoming more and more dated with the passage of time. Entrepreneurs, grown complacent with success, regarded technological change, once the life-blood of industry's expansion, with fear, suspicion or contempt.

Cotton

Cotton was the pacemaker and pioneer of industrial advance. It had introduced steam-powered, factory-organised production techniques to the rest of British industry. Between 1820 and 1840 it reached the peak of its relative importance in the economy, though, surprisingly, it did not complete the transition to full mechanisation in all stages of its production until the end of that period. Substantial numbers of handloom weavers still existed even in the 1850s and 1860s.

By that time the technology of the industry had fossilised, and developments, like ring-spinning, bypassed Lancashire mills, though the new machinery was being manufactured in Oldham itself. The industry survived because of:

1. The external economies which had been created by its expansion and concentration, for example the presence of specialised commodity exchanges, suppliers of textile machinery, subsidiary industries like bleaching and dyeing, and the services of shipping agents and a transport system which facilitated the supply of fuel and raw materials.

2. A flexible policy of switching markets, rather than of modifying products, though there was a tendency to concentrate on finer counts and more complex designs as the century wore on. In the early years, Europe was the main market; as it industrialised and became self-sufficient in cotton, British manufacturers, dependent on maintaining export levels for their prosperity, pushed into India (wiping out the native handcraft industry in the 1830s) and developed the U.S.A. By the end of the century the Empire, Africa, South America and the Far East were taking their place.

In terms of staving off the inevitable – recapitalisation – the industry can be said to have been successful. But it was blind to the embryonic challenge posed by Japan, and in the last great cotton boom, the twenty years before the Great War, Lancashire enthusiastically raised large sums of money through new joint-stock concerns – and invested them in the same machinery, confident that they could go on finding markets for the same goods.

Coal

Coal production rose continually throughout the nineteenth century, reaching a peak of output in 1913 (287,000,000 tons). Demand was strong in the first half of the century as industry began to switch to steam technology and the railways absorbed coal directly as fuel and indirectly through their demand for iron and bricks. In the 1850s and 1860s the upward trend was sustained by booming exports of iron and engineering products, plus rising consumption for gas and the domestic hearth. Exports of coal itself began to expand rapidly from this period, as Continental industry adopted steam, and shipping needed anthracite for bunkering. By the first decade of the twentieth century, one-third of coal output was being exported, and coal accounted for nearly 10 per cent of total British exports. (It also had the added advantage of providing a bulk outward freight, saving ships from going in ballast and thus keeping freight rates down.)

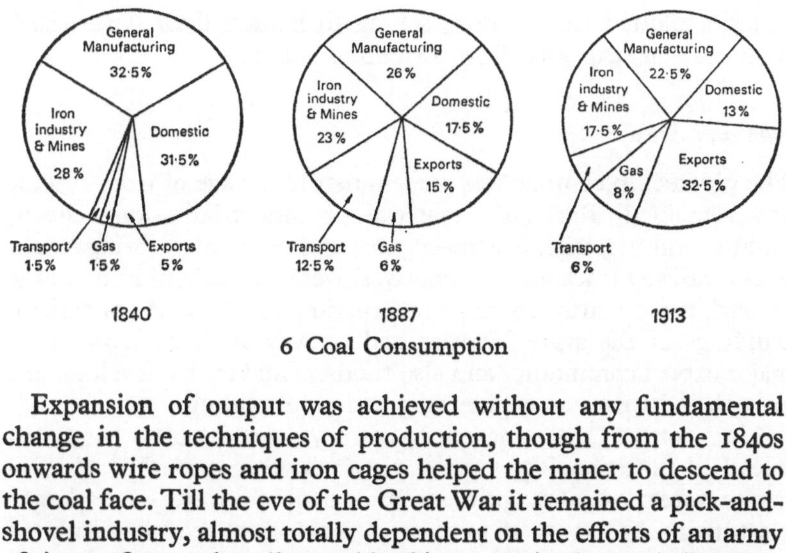

6 Coal Consumption

Expansion of output was achieved without any fundamental change in the techniques of production, though from the 1840s onwards wire ropes and iron cages helped the miner to descend to the coal face. Till the eve of the Great War it remained a pick-and-shovel industry, almost totally dependent on the efforts of an army of sinewy figures, kneeling and hacking away in the semi-darkness. Only by constantly enlarging the labour force, therefore, could expansion of output be maintained. The isolation of most mining communities and the prolific fertility of the miners, who reached their peak earnings young and married early, ensured that the supply of labour was forthcoming. In 1850 there were 200,000 miners; by 1880, 500,000; by 1914, 1,200,000. The price was paid in terms of falling productivity – output per man shift reached its zenith in 1880–4, and declined thereafter. But as world demand rose by 4 per cent per annum, rising costs could be passed on to the consumer.

British colliery owners, therefore, felt able to ignore the warnings of the economist, Jevons, that the coal seams were becoming increasingly inaccessible. In America, where seams were rich and labour scarce, by 1900 25 per cent of coal was being cut automatically and conveyed to the surface by belts. In Britain the percentage was negligible. The management of the coal industry apparently preferred to squander its energies in futile disputes with the powerful National Union of Miners.

The most damaging example of the lack of enterprise which pervaded the industry was the failure to develop the potential of coal by-products and derivatives. Aniline dyes, for instance, had been invented by Perkin, an Englishman, in the 1850s, and in the British textile industries a massive market lay to hand. But it was Germany which exploited this market, selling to Britain dyes synthesised from coal-tar, exported from Britain as waste!

Iron and Steel

The nineteenth century was pre-eminently the age of iron. It was, and remained, the basic material of industrialisation – cheap, durable and versatile. Steam-engines and machinery, bridges and docks, railway track and locomotives, were all made of iron, and it figured prominently in the construction of those characteristic buildings of the age – factories and railway stations. Iron was a major export commodity and also fundamental to the development of such industries as engineering and shipbuilding.

Like cotton, the nineteenth-century iron industry was bequeathed its technology by the previous generation. Its achievements were those of magnitude rather than of novelty – ever larger blast furnaces rather than new insights into the chemistry of metals. Only Neilson's hot air blast furnace (1829), which opened up the black-band ironstone of the Lowlands and raised Scotland's share of British iron output from 5 per cent to 25 per cent in twenty years, can be regarded as a breakthrough. Nevertheless the growth of the industry was spectacular – as evidence, for instance, by the rise of the iron-making town of Middlesborough; in 1821 it just did not exist, by 1901 it had a population of 91,000.

The major achievement of nineteenth-century metallurgy was the creation of a bulk steel industry, which, in half a century, overshadowed iron itself. Steel had long been renowned for its lightness and toughness, but in the early nineteenth century it was still an expensive product, difficult and costly to manufacture. Output was limited to some 40,000 tons annually (as opposed to some 3,000,000 tons of iron in 1850). Most of this was directed to the manufacture of those goods which required a fine cutting-edge – cutlery, razors and machine tools. Then between 1856 and 1879, the industry was revolutionised by three inventions:

1. Sir Henry Bessemer's 'converter' (1856), which immediately halved costs of steel production and made bulk output practicable. (The railway boom of the 1860s provided a convenient initial market to stimulate investment in the new process.)

2. The Siemens–Martin 'open-hearth' furnace (1864) which made it possible to improve quality control by more accurate heat regulation, and also enabled manufacturers to recycle scrap steel as a raw material. (The North-East, where such 'waste' was a by-product of the shipbuilding and engineering industries thus found this process an extremely attractive one.)

3. The Gilchrist-Thomas 'basic' process (1875) which enabled manufacturers, for the first time, to use low-grade phosphoric ores. The chief beneficiary here was not Britain, which had built up a commitment to Swedish high-grade imports, but Germany, which could now plunder the iron-fields of its newly acquired provinces of Alsace and Lorraine.

The net effect of these inventions, coupled with the demand from railways and steam-shipping (which adopted steel rapidly in the late 1870s and early 1880s) was to raise output to an annual average of 486,000 tons in the years 1871–4, a figure which was all but quadrupled in the next decade and reached 7,007,000 tons by 1910–14. Novel uses were found for steel, which had never before been so cheap or so abundant – bridges and steel-framed buildings are obvious examples.

The performance of the British steel industry was, however, by no means satisfactory. By the turn of the century Britain had been surpassed in output by Germany and the U.S.A., both industrial giants able to take advantage of vast natural resources and rising populations. As late-comers they profited from Britain's mistakes and equipped themselves with the latest integrated plant. The pioneer of steel continued to make do with a 'patch and mend' policy which led the American steel magnate, Andrew Carnegie, to condemn the equipment of the industry in the 1890s as being twenty years behind the times. British entrepreneurs who had rushed to take up the Bessemer and Siemens–Martin processes in the 1860s and 1870s, now found themselves burdened with obsolescent plant which they were unwilling to part with.

In part this was due to the family structure of many firms which made managements reluctant to write off plant which was technically still serviceable, though economically inefficient, perhaps because they regarded it almost as a form of personal property – an attitude which made objective cost accountancy more difficult. As in cotton, where the same criticism applies, many manufacturers took refuge in the production of highly specialised versions of the basic product (plates, pipes, angles) a policy which made Britain, on the eve of the Great War, the world's greatest *importer* of steel.

Engineering

Engineering owed its birth to industrialisation. A sprawling complex of sub-industries, with no definable core, it combined the traditions and skills of the millwright, the watchmaker and the maker of scientific and navigational instruments to grow amoeba-like, as a by-product of the expansion of particular activities such as coal-mining, cotton-spinning, iron-smelting and railway construction. By the mid-nineteenth century it had arrived, and its Founding Fathers – Bramah (inventor of the hydraulic press, the improved water-closet and the beer-tap), Maudslay (inventor of the screw-cutting lathe and the slide-rest) and Nasmyth (inventor of the steam hammer and pile-driver) – were immortalised in the pages of Samuel Smiles's *Lives of the Engineers* and *Industrial Biography*.

In the second half of the century the industry maintained its standards of technical excellence, despite the weaknesses of the British educational system. But it failed abysmally on the marketing side. In marine engineering and armaments, the reputation of British firms remained supreme, but in the vital (for the rest of industry) field of machine-tools Britain lost ground to Germany, whose manufacturers were willing to offer a more limited range of products at a far lower price. Rather than pay a British firm to produce a specialised machine for a particular task, manufacturers began to find it worth their while to restyle the production process to fit the capabilities of existing, but cheaper, machinery. British engineering was dogged by craftsmen's antiquated attitudes in an age of mass-production.

Conclusions

It was inevitable that new industrial rivals would one day emerge to challenge Britain's supremacy, the more so as she had liberally assisted them with profitable loans of her own technology, labour and capital. Given their resources and populations, it was likely that the U.S.A. and Germany would outstrip Britain in gross volume of output; but the sluggishness of Britain's response to this challenge, and her unwillingness to cast off both the plant and the attitudes which she had inherited from the pioneers of industrialism, made her relative decline greater than it might otherwise have been.

One explanation, at least as far as the staple industries are concerned, may lie in the family structure of British industry. Managerial talent is not necessarily hereditary and the family 'board' may be unwilling to incorporate outside talent or question accepted practices. Growth may even be regarded with apprehension, as disturbing the even tenor of established ways. Among the second and third generations, public school education and a desire to gain social acceptance, encouraged men to divert profits into land (for status) or foreign investments (for security) rather than back into the firm itself. 'The firm' was considered more as an estate which could provide a steady income, than a productive enterprise out of which a fortune could be made.

Other restraining factors were structural and institutional:

1. There was a division in some industries (notably cotton and engineering) between the man who made the product and the man who sold it. This may have hampered adaptation to changing market needs.

2. Banks were geared to the provision of short-term credits for trade and the Stock Exchange to long-term credits for railways, foreign governments or public utilities. Neither regarded raising capital for industry as a significant aspect of their functions – an attitude which was a legacy of the self-financing phase of industrial enterprise and which helped to reinforce that threadbare tradition of self-reliance.

3. The relative abundance of certain factors of production inhibited interest in new techniques. Whereas the relative cheapness of skilled labour in engineering retarded the adoption of more automatic machinery in Britain, in the U.S.A. the scarcity of such labour gave manufacturers an additional incentive to such

innovation. Similarly the cheapness of coal retarded the use of electricity in both metallurgy and manufacturing industry.

THE GROWTH INDUSTRIES

The 'growth industries', which have been the pace-makers of twentieth-century industry, originated in the nineteenth century. The most noticeable characteristic of their progress in Britain was that they failed to grow:

1. Electricity, for instance, owed much of its early development to England – Faraday's pioneering work in electromagnetism in the 1820s, Wheatstone's in electric telegraphy in the 1830s. Swan had begun work on the problem of an incandescent lamp in the 1840s, and a submarine telegraph cable was laid under the English Channel in 1851 and under the Atlantic in 1866. Yet in 1913 the output of the British electrical goods industry was only one-third of that of Germany, and exports about one-half. In the production of generating gear and telephone equipment and in the new field of radio, the U.S.A. and Germany had established a clear lead. When an electric underground railway system was begun in London between 1900 and 1914, it was largely American-equipped and financed. Undoubtedly it was the cheapness and availability of coal and gas in Britain which underlay the failure to develop this new form of power.

2. In chemicals, Britain had once held the foremost position, producing large quantities of chlorine (for textile bleaching), alkalis and sulphuric acid, but it was slow to take up organic chemistry and exploit the derivatives of coal and oil. By 1913 her proportion of world output was only 11 per cent, while Germany accounted for 24 per cent and the U.S.A. for 34 per cent. The leading British chemists were either trained in Germany or worked under German chemists in England. When the industry underwent a 'renaissance' in the twentieth century, it was under the pressure of war and under the leadership of the German-born Sir Ludwig Mond, founder of Brunner-Mond, the moving spirit in the formation of Imperial Chemical Industries.

3. In motor vehicles, the main pioneers were France and Germany, mutually obsessed with the military value of the internal combustion engine. The U.S.A., with its plentiful supplies of motor fuel and high-income mass-market for transport services, was the first to begin large-scale production. In Britain the railways

reached maximum efficiency in this period and also formed a powerful lobby against the development of other forms of motive power. Nevertheless, the Red Flag Act (1865) which required a man with a red warning flag to walk before all 'horseless carriages', was repealed in 1896. (An event celebrated then, and subsequently, by a rally drive from London to Brighton.) By 1914 Britain had no less than 200 firms producing motor vehicles and engineers like Lanchester had already made important contributions to the technology of motor transport. But most cars were 'custom-built', that is, hand-made and built to order. Standards of technical excellence were high, but productivity was low with most firms producing less than one car per man per annum. As a consequence one-third of domestic requirements were met by imports, largely from France and the United States.

Innovation and growth lagged most in those industries where science played the largest part. Britain clung obstinately to her traditions of empiricism, respect for the insights of the lone, gifted amateur rather than the systematic data produced by trained teams of research workers. (The former tended to be an eccentric and self-supporting aristocrat, the latter required financial resources beyond most British firms, which were small and unwilling to finance experimental work which would either turn up no useful result or benefit their rivals as much as themselves.)

In 1872 there were twelve men at Cambridge reading natural sciences, most intending to become doctors of medicine. At the same date there were eleven technical universities in Germany and the Massachusetts Institute of Technology had already celebrated its tenth anniversary. The first state grant for science education in Britain was not made until 1890. Public schools and universities doggedly emphasised the value of the classics, theology and 'pure' mathematics, thus starving industry of scientists and technologists and encouraging the ambitious sons of manufacturing dynasties to regard trade as vulgar. As a result Britain had a fine civil service and liberal professions of distinction, but Germany had the scientists (the optical/photographics combine, Zeiss, was practically an outgrowth of the University of Jena) and America had the dynamic men of enterprise.

The result was a deceleration of the economy's key sector; industrial production and investment, and the rate of growth of manufactured exports all fell. As Professor Mathias has written:

> This failure of new sectors to come forward rapidly at this time to take the place of traditional staple industries under challenge from abroad proved one of the most strategic weaknesses of the time and one of the most potentially damaging for the future (*The First Industrial Nation*).

FURTHER READING

G. C. Allen, *British Industries and their Organisation* (London, Longmans, 1951) contains narrative chapters on all major industries and a chapter outlining the growth of the industrial sector as a whole.

P. Deane and W. A. Cole, *British Economic Growth, 1688–1959* (Cambridge University Press, 1969) contains a valuable discussion of the growth of the staple industries.

A. L. Levine, *Industrial Retardation in Britain, 1880–1914* (London, Weidenfeld and Nicolson, 1967) examines the causes of technological stagnation in the latter half of the period.

H. J. Habakkuk, *American and British Technology in the Nineteenth Century* (Cambridge University Press, 1967) deals with the general problem of innovation.

S. G. Checkland, *The Rise of Industrial Society in England, 1815–85* (London, Longmans, 1964), Chapters 3 and 4, and P. Mathias, *The First Industrial Nation, 1700–1914* (London, Methuen, 1969), Chapters 5 and 15, contain full bibliographies of books and articles relating to particular industries and regions, and discuss more general questions such as innovation and the role of the entrepreneur.

C. Singer *et al.* (eds), *A History of Technology* (Oxford University Press, 1954–8), Volumes 4 and 5, studies industrial technology in detail.

T. K. Derry and T. I. Williams, *A Short History of Technology from Earliest Times to 1900* (Oxford University Press, 1960) studies industrial technology more briefly.

B. R. Mitchell and P. Deane, *An Abstract of British Historical Statistics* (Cambridge University Press, 1962) contains statistics of output, etc., for all major industries.

Chapter 5

AGRICULTURE

ITS ROLE IN THE INDUSTRIAL REVOLUTION

The critical role of agriculture in the process of industrialisation is often underestimated, or ignored, as though agricultural development was in no way related to the growth of industry and the expansion of population. In fact, agriculture performed the following valuable functions during the stages of 'take-off' and 'the drive to industrial maturity':

1. It supplied food for a rapidly expanding population without causing it to lower its living standard to any considerable extent, and without absorbing any large extra portion of that population in the task of providing food.

2. It supplied organic raw materials to a number of growing domestic industries:

(i) Wool – for textiles (Australia did not contribute significantly until the second half of the nineteenth century).
(ii) Hides – for shoes, harnesses, furniture.
(iii) Tallow – for candles, soap.
(iv) Grain – for baking (a growth industry in the larger towns) and brewing (a pioneer industry in the adaptation of steam power).
(v) Other material such as flax (for linen), horn, bones and straw (plaited into hats and baskets).

3. Landowners, newly prosperous from rising rent-rolls and eager to increase their incomes by reaching new markets, invested in numerous transport improvements, notably turnpike trusts and, to a lesser extent, canals. Those formed the infrastructure for industrial growth though no such conscious purpose was behind them originally. Landowners also used agricultural profits to develop coal and mineral deposits on their estates.

4. Finally landowners and farmers, numerically strong and individually wealthy, offered a sizable market for the sturdy

products of the new industrial England – clothes, crockery, cutlery, hardware and household linen. As a ballad (*c.* 1820) observed:

> If you'd seen the farmers 'wives' bout fifty years ago,
> In home-spun russet linsey clad from top to toe;
> But now a-days the farmers' wives are so puffed up with pride,
> In a dandy habit and green veil unto the market they must ride.

By the beginning of the nineteenth century, therefore, the English countryside had begun to take on its accustomed aspect, both physically and socially. *Physically*, in that it was divided into a chequer-board of compact, hedged fields, intersected by metalled roads. *Socially* in that landownership had become concentrated in a few hands. Some few thousands of landlords owned the land, some tens of thousands of farmers leased it from them and employed as labour a rural proletariat numbering close on a million. Agriculture was a capitalist field of enterprise, fully geared to the demands of the market. When Gregory King constructed his picture of English society in 1689, he distinguished a separate class of small owner-occupiers, farming largely for their own subsistence. His successor, Patrick Colquhoun, performing the same exercise a century and a quarter later, ignored them as a negligible factor. The consequence, at least to contemporaries, was less obviously higher productivity in agriculture, than an appalling increase in rural poverty. The Reverend D. Davies observed that:

> The practice of enlarging and engrossing of farms, and especially that of depriving the peasantry of all landed property, have contributed greatly to increase the number of dependent poor. . . . Thus an amazing number of people have been reduced from a comfortable state of partial independence to the precarious conditions of hirelings, who, when out of work, must immediately come to their parish [for poor relief] (*The Case of the Labourers in Husbandry Truly Stated 1795*).

In fact the major cause of rural poverty and unemployment was rural overpopulation and the immobility of a rustic labour force burdened by ignorance, illiteracy, tied cottages, large families and fear of losing localised rights of poor relief.

THE STATE OF AGRICULTURE IN 1815

During the Napoleonic wars agriculture had prospered. The

farmers' toast 'A bad harvest or a bloody war' became proverbial. In fact, the high grain prices of those years were due to a combination of circumstances, chiefly a number of years of successive bad harvests and the demands of a rapidly rising and increasingly urban (i.e. non-food-producing) population. Nearly half a million men were under arms and required to be fed, as did a number of our allies and the horses of the combatants.

In this atmosphere of agricultural euphoria many farmers were encouraged to try out the new methods of cultivation they had formerly regarded with scepticism – enclosure, crop-rotation, selective breeding. A General Enclosure Act was passed in 1801 to speed up the process. Many agriculturalists (especially the smaller ones) took out mortgages to finance their improvements – a policy which placed them heavily in debt and, in fact, assumed that the artificially high prices of war-time would continue indefinitely. They did not.

There was a bumper harvest in 1813 and, to the perceptive, it became clear that English agriculture had turned the corner towards over-production. By extending the margin of cultivation and adopting the latest techniques of intensive husbandry, English farmers had now outrun the capacity of even the large and expanding domestic market to absorb all they produced. Not until the 1830s were the two to come into equilibrium once more, and in the meantime English farmers were preoccupied with the fear that the cessation of hostilities against France would mean an open door to a flood of cheap Continental grain. Frantic in their desire to safeguard the capital which they had quite literally sunk into the soil, they demanded protection from Parliament – and got it.

THE CORN LAW OF 1815

The essential decree of the celebrated Corn Law was that no foreign wheat might be sold in England (though it could be imported and stored – a loop-hole which the speculators made full use of) until the price of home-grown wheat reached 80*s*. a quarter, the price which the agricultural interest reckoned necessary to give a fair return on their invested capital and enable the amortised to meet their interest payments. Similar arrangements, with different price levels, were made for other grains, like barley and oats.

Naturally, such a measure had a very direct bearing on the cost of living (bread accounted for perhaps 70–80 per cent of a labourer's weekly expenditure) and there were many protests against it. The City of Westminster, for instance, petitioned that it would cause:

> considerable inconvenience to the middle orders of society; great distress to the poorer and more numerous classes; a most serious injury to the manufactures and commerce of the country; a great loss of national property; a powerful inducement to emigration; and eventually, though not immediately, a bar to the prosperity of the landed interest itself.

Such protests fell on deaf ears when addressed to a Parliament composed of landowners and their nominees. Besides which, they could easily convince themselves that what was good for agriculture was good for Britain. Agriculture after all employed one-third of the labour force and contributed one-third of the national income. It was, therefore, vital to the economic and social stability of the state.

The Corn Law was, however, fundamentally irrelevant to Britain's agricultural problems, because it failed to take account of the essential factors in the situation:

1. Imports at this time, given the state of shipping and the available areas of supply, could only account for 5 per cent or at most 15 per cent of the nation's needs.

2. British agriculture, by adopting the latest methods of production, had raised itself to new levels of productivity which could not be abandoned.

3. Grain prices are basically determined by the fortunes of the harvest, which depends on the weather. And you cannot legislate for the weather.

Agriculture, therefore, was in for a rough time.

THE PROBLEMS OF POST-WAR AGRICULTURE

Superimposed on the structural problem of periodic chronic over-supply, there were more transitory burdens – chiefly the task of absorbing a large proportion of the 300,000 servicemen discharged after the defeat of Napoleon. These had to be accommodated alongside a labour force which was already chafing under the demoralisation of the Speenhamland system of poor relief and the vicious penalties for poaching imposed by the new Game Laws.

For the farmer this all meant higher poor rates, in addition to mortgage repayments. The wild fluctuations of grain prices in the early post-war years made budgeting difficult, but the abolition of war-time Malt Tax in 1816 eased the position a little. Nevertheless, these years saw a definite weeding-out of smaller men, much to the disgust of contemporaries like William Cobbett, the radical journalist, whose *Rural Rides* showed a keen knowledge of rural life. Cobbett blamed the stock-jobbers, paper money and the crushing burden of the vastly inflated National Debt. The consequence he believed was that:

> Instead of families of small farmers with all their exertions, all their decency of dress and of manners, and all their scrupulousness as to character, we have *families of paupers*. . . .

As for the labourers, they had touched rock-bottom. Cobbett angrily invited his readers to

> Go down into the villages . . . and then look at the miserable sheds in which the labourers reside. Look at these hovels, made of mud and straw, bits of glass, or old cast-off windows. . . . Enter them and look at the bits of chairs or stools; the wretched boards tacked together to serve for a table, . . . and survey the rags on the backs of the wretched inhabitants.

In the long, hot summer of 1830 the wretched inhabitants rose in revolt. Co-ordinated (or so the fear-ridden landlords believed), by some mysterious 'Captain Swing', they indulged in a guerrilla campaign of rick-burning, machine-smashing and intimidation. The hanging of 9 men and the transportation for life of 457 others put a stop to this agitation which covered the whole of the agricultural South from Kent to Dorset to East Anglia.

Not unnaturally, threatened by bankruptcy and their labourers alternately, the farmers and landlords turned to Parliament for relief. A number of measures were obtained:

1. Revisions of the Corn Law and the introduction of sliding-scales of duty in 1822, 1828 and 1842.

2. The New Poor Law of 1834, which cut the Gordian knot of Speenhamland and, by the principle of 'less eligibility', attempted to force the surplus labourer into an unaccustomed occupational mobility.

3. The Tithe Commutation Act (1836), which rationalised the customary annual payments to the established church.

4. General Enclosure Acts (1836 and 1845), which enabled farmers to mop up the last remaining areas of common and 'waste'.

THE STRUGGLE FOR THE CORN LAWS

In 1838 the Anti-Corn Law League was founded in Manchester. Its birth-place was no matter of chance. 'Cottonopolis' was the capital of British manufacturing industry – industry which depended on export markets for its prosperity. The middle-class merchants and manufacturers of the city, still smarting under the imposition of a Factory Act (1833) cast upon them by an unholy alliance of radicals and landowning reactionaries, were out to attack the privileged position of British agriculture in the name of *laissez-faire*. In a sense it was also an aspect of the general attack on the remnants of feudal England and aristocratic privilege which the Great Reform Act (1832) had presaged and which the Northcote–Trevelyan Report on the Civil Service was to consummate.

The Anti-Corn Law League presented the case for repeal with considerable flair and a great deal of self-righteous indignation, both put over by the latest techniques available – steam-printed leaflets, newsletters (thanks to the Penny Post) and mass-meetings (thanks to the railway) addressed by masters of rhetoric such as Richard Cobden and John Bright. It was a two-faced movement. The working poor were told that repeal of the Corn Laws would bring them cheap bread. Audiences of manufacturers were assured that the same measure would enable them to force down wages and sell more, on a reciprocal basis, to those agricultural nations from whom we should purchase our bread corn.

In the event it was Nature that determined for repeal. Peel, the Prime Minister and leader of the landowning Tory party, was also the son of a millionaire cotton merchant and, in time, was won over by the arguments of the League. But arguments are one thing and action is another. It took a catastrophe – the Irish famine of 1845–6 – to push him towards the fatal step. The failure of the Irish potato crop, the starvation of a million people and the emigration of a million more, induced him to repeal the Corn Laws in 1846 in the hope that a flood of foreign grain would sweep in to relieve famine, or at least prevent revolution. It did the latter, but not the former, and it split his party for twenty years. The small farmers, particularly those who depended heavily or wholly on grain, screamed 'traitor' and resisted repeal to the last. But without the great landlords they were leaderless, and the great landlords expected to gain from railways, urban rents and mineral workings what they lost from wheat-farming. The dairy and stock breeders, too, stood aside, confident of demand for their products, safe from imports, and hoping cheap grain would mean lower feed costs for them and higher sales of meat and butter to the worker who could get his bread cheaply.

HIGH FARMING – THE GOLDEN AGE

The repeal of the Corn Laws was expected to usher in a period of unparalleled depression. In fact it did the reverse. Why?

Firstly, the productivity of British agriculture was continuing to rise because:

1. There was a better understanding of the part to be played by science. Liebig's work on organic chemistry in agriculture was published in 1840 and the Rothamsted experimental station established two years later. The annual shows of the Royal Agricultural Society (established 1838) helped to spread a knowledge of new techniques and implements. Iron and steel implements, now cheaper and more efficient, came into more general use.

2. Fertilizer began to play a major role in raising yields and restoring soil fertility. Super-phosphates were manufactured artificially. Bones were imported from the Continent, nitrates from Chile, guano from Peru (none in 1840 – over 200,000 tons in 1847). To F. M. L. Thompson, this development symbolises a new, rational attitude towards food production, a determination to regard the farm as a processing centre rather than a fully self-enclosed unit and community. He has, therefore, christened this period a 'second agricultural revolution'.

3. Drainage became popular on heavy clay soils, widening the range of potential crops and diminishing labour requirements. The invention of the mole plough and Scragg's tile-pipe made machine-made drainage technically feasible, while the subsidies announced in Peel's 'Repeal' speech and the loans made available to farmers by mortgage-brokers, made such projects financially viable. Sir John Clapham estimated that 4 to 5 millon acres of land were thus improved, at a cost of about £20,000,000 in the quarter century after repeal.

4. Implements remained fairly simple, however. Steam-

threshing was used mainly by the self-consciously 'progressive' farmer. Veterinary science all but stood still.

The second major factor behind British agricultural prosperity was a buoyant domestic market:

1. Population was still rising rapidly and, for the first time, substantial numbers of wage-earners were enjoying a rise in real incomes.

2. Railways made possible cheaper transit over longer distances, rapid collection and delivery of perishable commodities such as fresh milk and fruit, and swift returns of cheap lime, fertiliser machinery and building materials.

Farmers prospered in these years, but at the cost of heavy investment in buildings, drainage, prize stock and new implements. This capital-intensive approach was what Sir James Caird had called for in his pamphlet *High Farming . . . the Best Substitute for Protection* (1848), but it was based on the assumption that the market would remain buoyant. But it did not – in the long run.

For a quarter of a century, however, the sun shone on the British farmer, both literally and metaphorically. He could view with equanimity the acceleration of the flight from the land: 300,000 men left farming between 1851 and 1871, and for the first time the numbers employed began to fall *absolutely* as well as relatively. But the farmer was safe. There was no possibility of massive imports of foreign grain or meat. The railway had not yet penetrated the Prairie or the Pampas. In 1850 four-fifths of Britain's imported grain came from Europe, and Europe had little enough to spare. Shipping was still slow, sail-powered and unrefrigerated. Britain still produced half of her wheat and six-sevenths of her meat. Well might her farmers be content.

THE DEPRESSION IN AGRICULTURE

Disaster was, as ever, lurking around the corner. The 1870s marked a turning-point. In Britain there was an unparalleled run of bad weather, bringing catastrophic harvests, foot and mouth disease and liver rot. For the first time, grain, and later meat, began to come in quantity from the newly-tilled, fertile and temperate lands beyond the Atlantic and the Indian Ocean. The United States, Argentina, Canada, Australia, New Zealand and Russia, were all brought within the orbit of Britain's trade, by the railway and the compound-engine, and the refrigerated steam-ship. Under the impact of the new transport technology, freight rates fell dramatically. The price of transferring a quarter of wheat from Chicago to Liverpool fell from 11*s*. to 3*s*. between 1870 and 1900. By the latter date 67 per cent of Britain's imported grain was coming from beyond Europe.

Royal Commissions were appointed to survey the depressed state of British agriculture. Their reports are both pessimistic and misleading. Prices and rents *were* falling sharply, in some cases by 30–40 per cent, but the members of the Commissions were appointed by a Parliament still dominated by the South of England.

Crop Acreage and Livestock in Great Britain, 1872 and 1913

	1872	1913
Crops (thousands of acres)		
Market gardens	232	365
Fallow, grass and pasture	17,349	21,933
Root crops	3,631	2,953
Wheat	3,599	1,756
Other corns	5,975	5,166
Livestock (thousands)		
Cattle	5,625	6,964
Sheep	27,922	23,931
Pigs	2,772	2,234

Source: B. R. Mitchell and P. Deane, *Abstract of British Historical Statistics* (Cambridge University Press, 1962).

They equated agriculture with wheat-farming and assumed that the problems of a corn county like Essex were general ones. In fact much of British agriculture was not faring too badly. The dairy and stock farmers benefited from the low cost of imported feeds and the increased demand (now that bread was cheap) for meat, cheese and butter.

RE-ADJUSTMENT

Re-adjustment came slowly. Structural changes are never easily comprehended by their victims. It takes a long time to realise that one is not simply enduring the worst-ever in a series of recurrent depressions. When they did see the score, British farmers knew they must sell out or soldier on. Those who chose the latter course went in for the products with which imports could not seriously compete:

1. Fresh milk – for urban centres and the food-processing industries. 6,000,000 acres of pasture were added between 1866 and 1911.
2. Prime meat and poultry.
3. Fruit – particularly for the new jam-making industry. Kent and the Vale of Evesham led the way here.
4. Vegetables and market gardening – around the perimeters of large cities. Cheshire, for instance served Manchester and the Potteries, Hertfordshire and Middlesex served London.

Wheat, formerly the most important single crop, dwindled to insignificance. In 1874 it accounted for 3,600,000 acres, by 1900 half that.

Ever-improving railway services and the fact that 'the sort of man who had bread and cheese for his dinner forty years ago now demands a chop' (written in 1899) helped agriculture find a new place in the industry state. But it was a smaller place, despite the fact that the value of the industry's output rose 10 per cent during this difficult period. The labour force was still shrinking (1871 – 962,000; 1901 – 621,000) and protection was, as Disraeli had said, 'not only dead but damned'. It was the author of this famous phrase who, as Tory Prime Minister (1874–80), presided over the first stages of agriculture's ruin and did nothing to stop the rot. Free Trade was now the City's sacred cow and it meant cheap bread to the urban voters he had himself enfranchised in 1867. Electorally, the farmers had lost their old influence and so could no longer turn to Parliament for aid and protection.

The result was that by the turn of the century agriculture contributed less to the national income than foreign investment (6 per cent as against 7 per cent). Well over half our basic foodstuffs were now imported; the strategic as well as the economic vulnerability of such a situation may easily be imagined. Britain was now tied irrevocably to international trade for her very sustenance.

FURTHER READING

J. D. Chambers and G. E. Mingay, *The Agricultural Revolution, 1750–1880* (London, Batsford, 1969) is a very useful overall survey.

C. S. Orwin and E. H. Whetham, *A History of British Agriculture, 1846–1914* (London, Longmans, 1964) covers a shorter period in more detail.

E. L. Jones, *The Development of English Agriculture 1815–73* (London, Macmillan, 1968) is a useful pamphlet, but rather technical perhaps for beginners.

F. M. L. Thompson, *English Landed Society in the Nineteenth Century* (London, Routledge, 1963) looks at things from the top, while M. K. Ashly, *Life of Joseph Ashby of Tysoe* (Cambridge University Press, 1961) gives the viewpoint from the other end.

The Autobiography of Joseph Arch (London, MacGibbon, 1966) deals with the early life and later struggles of the first organiser of agricultural trade unions.

R. Jefferies, *Hodge and his Masters* (London, MacGibbon, 1966) contains masterly sketches of English rural types in the 1870s and 1880s.

John Burnett, *Plenty and Want* (Harmondsworth, Penguin, 1968) deals with both the production and the consumption of food since 1815.

Chapter 6

TRANSPORT

ROADS AND CANALS

Both roads and canals were the product of eighteenth-century enterprise, but they attained their peak of efficiency in the early nineteenth century, only to be swiftly rendered obsolete by the railways. Their contribution to the initial stages of industrialisation should not, however, be underestimated.

Roads

The deplorable state of English roads around 1700 was commented on by British travellers and foreign visitors alike. In an Act of 1555, each parish was made responsible for the upkeep of the roads within its boundaries, but as the inhabitants of most parishes saw no reason why they should maintain roads chiefly for the benefit of others, the roads continued to deteriorate. The device which came to their rescue was the turnpike trust, an association, usually of local landowners, who put up the money to lay down a section of good road (say from ten to twelve miles long) and then, having erected toll-gates at either end of it, levied a charge on all travellers who wished to use it.

Parliamentary initiative lay behind the first such venture, at Wadesmill, Hertfordshire, in 1663, but thereafter local initiatives were sufficient. By 1750 some 400 turnpike trusts had been formed; between 1751 and 1790 over 1600 were set up, and in the succeeding 40 years another 2,450. The main motive of the trustees was not to make a profit from the tolls they charged but to help the road pay for itself and to reap their own reward by reaching new markets for the produce of their estates at lower costs.

The turnpike trusts established the outlines of a national road system, which was immeasurably improved by the efforts of two engineers – Thomas Telford (engineer of the Glasgow–Carlisle Road and the London–Holyhead Road, Surveyor of Roads in

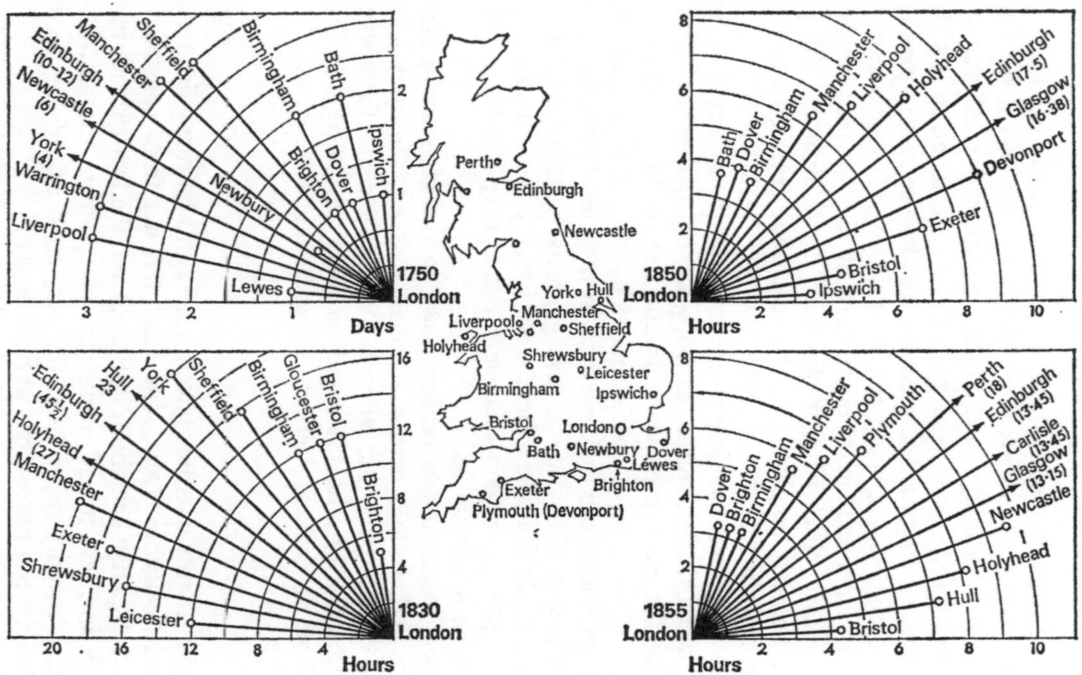

7 The Revolution of Speed: Times of Travel

Shropshire and first President of the Institution of Civil Engineers) and John Loudon Macadam, the populariser of a durable system of road surfacing, subsequently named after him.

The main results of improved roads were:

1. Land transport costs were reduced, in many cases by half. Overland haulage, however, remained too expensive for bulky goods, which went by water: Adam Smith estimated that what 6 men and 1 ship could take from Leith to London in few days, would need 50 wagons, 100 men and 400 horses to haul overland, and the journey would take a month or six weeks. Coastal shipping, therefore, remained an integral part of the *internal* transport system. Smith observed that one-third of all Britain's shipping was permanently employed in the coal trade from Newcastle to London and the East Coast ports.

2. Travel became possible all the year round, an immense boon to commerce. Mail-coaches, carrying letters and news, began in 1784 and the road improvements effected by Macadam and his followers slashed stage-coach times. In 1754 the journey from London to Edinburgh took ten days in summer, twelve in winter; by 1833 it was advertised as taking precisely 42 hrs 33 min. all year round. By that date there were some 3,000 coaches on the roads, employing 30,000 men, and connecting London with all the main provincial cities.

3. Rural isolation was broken down in the interests of labour mobility and a more perfect national market. This was a long process, completed by the railways. Western Ireland, for instance, still lacked roads in the 1820s and turnpike construction in Wales sparked off the famous 'Rebecca Riots' as late as 1843.

Canals

England's lengthy coastline (5,000 miles) and its many deep estuaries and navigable rivers, long inhibited her from constructing canals, such as had been built in France and the Netherlands in the sixteenth and seventeenth centuries. No point in the island was more than seventy miles from the sea, or, south of the border, more than fifteen miles from navigable water.

The quickening pace of economic life created transport bottlenecks which were overcome, in the 1720s, by river 'improvement' (dredging, straightening, removal of obstructions), and in the 1750s by the construction of the first canals, the Sankey Brook canal and the Duke of Bridgewater's canal from Worsley to Manchester. The success of these ventures led to two speculative 'manias' in the 1770s and 1790s, resulting in the construction of various 'trunk' canals of great length, linking rivers, ports and great cities. By the end of the century, London, Liverpool, Hull and Bristol were connected by a network of waterways of which Birmingham was the hub and focal point. Canal building then more or less ceased, apart from some government-sponsored projects, begun during the French wars for strategic purposes. The total length of the canal system was 2,200 miles (plus 2,000 miles of navigable river), and the cost, a modest £20,000,000.

The chief benefits conferred by canals were:

1. They provided a cheap form of transport for bulky goods, particularly coal (90 of the 165 Canal Acts passed between 1758 and 1802 had the carriage of coal as their main purpose) but also building-materials and food. The Bridgewater canal halved the price of coal in Manchester, a benefit to householders as well as to manufacturers. Cheap transport was an immense stimulus to industry: Lancashire and Yorkshire benefited greatly; the South Wales coal-fields were opened up by canals, and the land-locked West Midlands boomed as it broke through the barrier of transfer costs which had formerly limited its ability to compete in export markets. The ease and cheapness with which food and building-materials could now be brought facilitated urban growth.

2. The smoothness of water transport (vital for pottery), and the fact that canals could be used to provide water for steam-engines, cooling processes, etc., and to carry away effluent and waste products were a great help to industry.

3. Canals popularised the joint-stock company as a device for raising large sums of capital by mobilising the scattered resources of a multiplicity of small savers.

4. The actual work of construction stimulated the building-materials industries, generated employment for 'navvies' (originally 'navigators') and pioneered new techniques in civil engineering and labour management which were valuable precedents for the railway builders.

Canals did suffer from a number of disadvantages:

1. When built in wholly agricultural areas (e.g. the Kennet and Avon canal), they were unable to generate enough traffic to pay their way. Constructional difficulties limited their value in hilly areas.

2. As monopolies, they could be, and were, abused in the matter of tolls and charges.

3. They were not built as a system and the multiplicity of managements and gauges hindered the development of through-traffic.

4. Traffic was liable to delays caused by caused by floods, freezing and drought.

RAILWAYS

> The Romans were the great road-makers of the ancient world – the English are the great railroad makers of the modern world. The tramway was an English invention, the locomotive was the production of English genius and the first railways were constructed and carried to success in England.

R. D. Baxter's triumphant assertion of England's unique contribution to the development of railways was based on the assumption that they were the most important innovation of the age, as indeed they were. Before outlining their pervasive effect on every sector of the economy and every facet of national life, it is necessary to give a brief indication of the chronology of their construction:

1604 – earliest record of parallel tracks in England.

1767 – Coalbrookdale foundry laid down rails made of iron.

Late eighteenth century – extensive development of railways on Tyneside, most connecting pit-head workings to navigable water.

1804 – Richard Trevithick runs the first successful locomotive at Pen-y-darryn colliery.

1825 – Stockton and Darlington railway was opened. Coal shipments out of Stockton rise from 1,200 tons (1822) to 66,000 tons (1828) and 1,500,000 tons (1840).

1830 – Liverpool and Manchester Railway was opened – thirty-one miles of double-track involving a viaduct, a cutting and a tunnel with an uphill climb. The engineer for both these ventures was the self-educated George Stephenson.

1834–6 – the first 'railway mania' led to investment of some £50,000,000 in building trunk routes between Britain's major cities. A trade recession brought a temporary halt to speculation which was resumed in

1844–6 – a second 'railway mania'; a further expenditure of

£200,000,000 (much of which was wasted) completed the trunk routes. By 1850 6,000 miles of track were open.

Construction lagged in the 1850s, but there was another large spurt in the 1860s and for the rest of the century continual additions were made to the system, pushing out into the Highlands, Central Wales and East Anglia. Double-, triple- and quadruple-tracking, block-signalling, automatic-braking, and such refinements as corridors, lighting, heating and dining cars were all introduced after the 1870s. By 1911 the network had reached its greatest extent – some 24,000 miles.

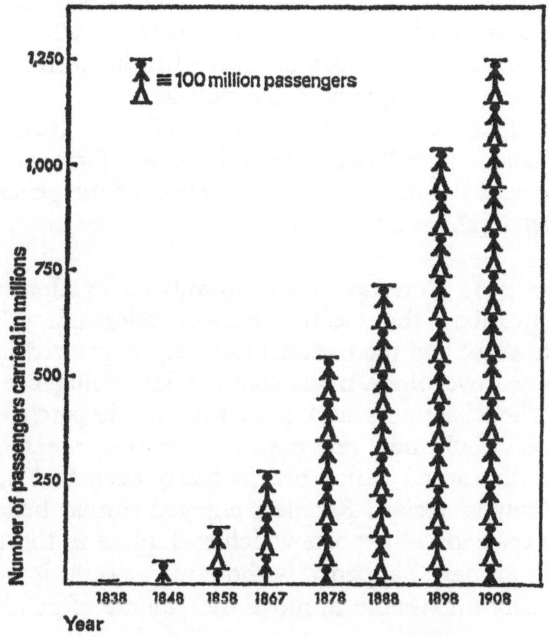

8 The Transport Revolution: Railways

The Impact of the Railways

Short-term. (1) Construction provided employment for armies of navvies (250,000–300,000 in the 1840s). By the 1850s 90,000 men were employed in running the railways. The building-materials industries, moreover, benefited from the enormous demand for bricks, stone, timber, glass and cement.

(2) Railways, through their demand for iron (rails, bridges, station furniture), engineering products (locomotives, rolling-stock) and coal (as fuel and indirectly via iron and bricks), lifted industrialisation into its second, heavy industry phase, just as the momentum supplied by the cotton industry was beginning to flag.

(3) Railways gave the death-blow to long-distance coaches, which vanished in a decade; as a consequence every single turnpike trust went bankrupt. Canals were too fragmented in their ownership to resist take-over bids by the railway companies which generally let them fall into decay. Some (e.g. around Birmingham) still survived because they came right up to the factory itself. Others were used to carry goods where speed was unimportant (e.g. sand). Coastal shipping lost some of its bulk traffic to railways. Horse transport *within* towns increased with the need for taxi and delivery services to complement the railway.

(4) The speculative manias stimulated the growth of the Stock Exchange, popularised the joint-stock form of company organisation and familiarised a wide section of the general public with the idea of share investment.

Long-term. (1) Commerce was stimulated by the new speed of communication: the electric railway telegraph (1837), the Penny Post (1840) and the national newspaper, printed in London and distributed overnight, made commercial intelligence instantly available. The cheapness and regularity of despatch on which manufacturers could now rely meant a lowering of real costs and a release of the capital which had formerly been tied up in large reserves of raw materials. Retailers enjoyed similar benefits. The enormous expansion of exports which took place in the 1850s and 1860s could not have happened without railways, as it would have been physically impossible to move the volume of goods without them.

(2) Agriculture benefited by reaching new urban markets. Lime, manure and fertilisers went to the farm at cheap rates; stock no longer had to walk to market. A new long-distance trade in perishables (milk, fruit, vegetables) became possible. The fishing industry made great use of this new facility: Hull, Grimsby and Yarmouth were able to expand their operations because they could now make daily deliveries of fresh fish to London and the great inland cities.

(3) Railways developed as an export product – railway iron,

locomotives and stock. Entrepreneurs like Thomas Brassey built railways all over the world using British materials, labour and capital.

(4) Urban growth was encouraged:

(i) generally – by the cheapness and ease with which necessities could be brought to towns and its products distributed;

(ii) specifically – by the growth of 'railway towns' which derived their *raison d'être* from the new form of transport (Crewe Swindon, Doncaster), by the rejuvenation of older settlements which attained a new significance as junctions (Rugby), and by the growth of seaside resort towns which depended on the railway for their trade (Blackpool, Brighton, Bournemouth and Eastbourne).

In the later years of the century the shape of towns changed as the extension of commuter services encouraged urban 'sprawl'.

(5) Among the innumerable social implications of railways were:

(i) Greenwich Mean Time was adopted over the whole country (to synchronise train timetables);

(ii) new architectural styles evolved (e.g. the functionalism of King's Cross) and new techniques (e.g. the use of iron spans and glass for roofs);

(iii) the townsmen's diet became more varied;

(iv) mass-meetings and 'whistle-stop' tours became a regular feature of politics (e.g. Anti-Corn Law League demonstrations for the former, Gladstone's 'Midlothian' campaign for the latter);

(v) the idea and habit of travel became more general. Holiday excursions became popular in the 1840s; seaside holidays from the 1860s and 1870s.

The boost which railways gave to the developing economy is well-illustrated by another of R. D. Baxter's observations:

> Increased facilities of transit led to increased trade; increased trade gave greater employment and improved wages; the dimunition in the cost of transit and the repeal of fiscal duties cheapened provisions; and the immense flood of commerce which set in since 1850 has raised the incomes and the prosperity of the working classes to an unprecedented height. Railways were the first cause of this great change and are entitled to share largely with free trade the glory of its subsequent increase and

of the national benefit ('Railway Extension and its Results', *Journal of the Royal Statistical Society* (1866) reprinted in *Essays in Economic History*, ed. E. M. Carus-Wilson, vol. 3).

SHIPPING

Whether considered as an economy or as a state, Britain has long regarded a strong shipping industry as essential to her vital interests. In 1700 the merchant fleet, which had successfully challenged the Dutch for the position of common carrier to the world, consisted of no less than 6,000 ships and employed 100,000

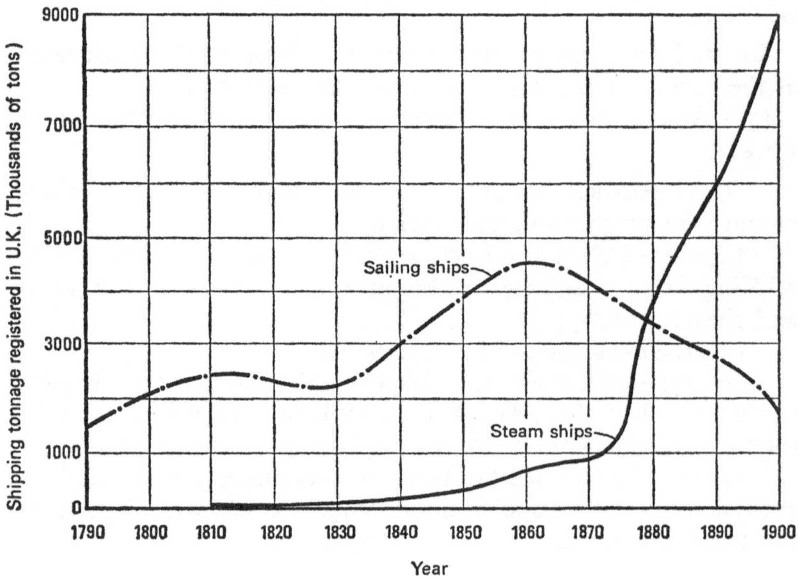

9 Shipping, 1790–1909

men, the largest occupational group after agriculture. Imperial expansion in the eighteenth century made shipping even more important, and the Navigation Acts, which reserved the trade of Britain and her colonies to British ships, were regarded as fundamental to the security and prosperity of the nation.

The emergence of a powerful American fleet in the early nineteenth century came as a shock and a challenge. For nearly half a century American shippers acted as pacemakers to the industry:

1. In 1816 the Black Ball Line (New York to Liverpool) introduced the idea of a 'liner' ship, sailing regularly on a fixed route at fixed times, regardless of whether it was full or empty and (as far as possible) regardless of the weather.

2. American ship-designers, notably Donald McKay, led the field, pioneering the 'clipper' type of long, sleek ship, which sailed faster and carried more but needed fewer men as crew.

3. The American shipbuilding industry (which had supplied one-third of British shipping in the eighteenth century) grew rapidly thanks to the plentiful supplies of timber to hand on the north-east coast of the United States.

Britain was hampered in her response by the fact that:

1. She was largely dependent on imported timber (from the Baltic and Canada).

2. The obsolete Tonnage Acts, which fixed harbour dues according to a formula, for calculating the volume of a ship, favoured slow, high-sided vessels.

3. The Navigation Acts cushioned inefficient shipowners against competition.

The abolition of the Tonnage Acts (1836) and the Navigation Laws (1849) allowed British shippers to emulate American designs and weeded out the less efficient managers. The discovery of gold in Australia (1848) simultaneously opened up a new and profitable long run. By 1860, however, the American merchant fleet had all but achieved parity with that of Great Britain, and had almost outstripped her in productivity and technical excellence. In the event, it was steam that came to the rescue.

Experiments to harness steam-power for shipping had been conducted by William Symington at the end of the eighteenth century, and his *Charlotte Dundas* had successfully shown its paces in 1802. Steam-ferries came into operation a decade later, valued for their ability to sail regularly against tidal flows and contrary winds and currents. By the 1820s, steam-ships were extensively employed around Britain's coast, across the Channel and the Irish Sea and as far away as Spain. In the following decade the first all-steam crossing of the Atlantic was achieved by *Sirius* (1838). I. K. Brunel's *Great Western* (which had followed *Sirius* on its epic run) was followed by the same engineer's *Great Britain* (1843), the first all-iron, all-steam, screw-propelled vessel.

His massive *Great Eastern* (1856) was a financial failure, but foreshadowed the technical triumphs that were to come.

Government mail-contracts, awarded to Cunard, the P. & O. and other steam navigation lines, were an important factor in keeping steam-shipping going in the 1840s and 1850s. The steamers offered greater regularity than a sailing-ship, but were no faster; in return they received what was, in effect, a government subsidy. Despite the advances that had been made in steam-ship design (iron hulls, screw-propellers) it seemed that the low thermal efficiency of their engines would prevent them from ever challenging the sailing-ship as a carrier of bulk cargo. Passengers and mail could easily be accommodated by them, but grain, timber or other such goods could never be transported at a reasonable freight-rate so long as the amount of fuel-space required by a steam-ship prevented it from having a large cargo capacity.

The technical breakthrough was made by Alfred Holt's perfected multiple-expansion 'compound' engine (1862). The fuel economies which it made possible revolutionised the design of steam-powered shipping. By 1865 more steam-ships than sailing-ships were being launched each year. In the late 1870s and early 1880s steel was widely and rapidly adopted as a basic shipbuilding material. In the 1890s Parson's steam turbine made its appearance.

The sailing-ship was slow to disappear altogether, although fewer were launched each year. Some were still in service in the 1930s. There were a number of reasons for this:

1. The wind was free – coal was not.

2. Sailing-ship design continued to improve (e.g. in the use of steel for hulls, masts and spars).

3. Improved charts, maps and books of sailing directions (giving details of favourable winds and currents) were issued on the basis of data collected by the U.S. and British Navies and various geographical societies. In many cases they cut sailing times by one-third or even a half.

4 On many long runs (e.g. bringing nitrates from Chile), the time-factor was of no importance.

5. Sailing-ships did not require an army of stokers to feed boilers and maintain trim; they could, therefore, manage with smaller, and consequently cheaper, crews.

The perfection of the steam-ship had important consequences for Britain:

1. The American challenge was decisively defeated. The distractions of the Civil War (1861–5) and the subsequent westward drive across the Prairies diverted American energies at a critical moment. In the production of steam-ships, Britain, with its developed iron, coal and engineering industries, had a comparative cost advantage such as the United States had enjoyed when wood had been the basic shipbuilding material. Now it was British ships which could carry more, faster and cheaper. Transatlantic trade became a British monopoly, while American shippers were confined to coastal waters. By 1890 Great Britain, with nearly half of world tonnage, had twice as much as America, eight times as much as Germany and ten times as much as France.

2. Shipping became one of the nation's greatest service industries, contributing over £100,000,000 per annum towards invisible exports by the turn of the century (sufficient alone to cover the standing deficit on merchandise trade). Substantial earnings from insurance and merchant banking services were directly related to this activity.

3. British exporters (i.e. most British manufacturers) found the world's most sophisticated distribution system at their disposal. Bulk importation of foodstuffs was also made possible and emigration and imperial development encouraged.

4. A great shipbuilding industry grew up on the estuaries of the Clyde, Tyne and Mersey. The strategic importance of this industry ensured that Britain retained a technical supremacy, which she lost in other industries after 1870. On the eve of the Great War, Britain still possessed more than 60 per cent of world shipbuilding capacity and 'second-hand' as well as new, ships were a valuable export. Steel, coal and engineering were all boosted by 'derived demand' effects from shipbuilding.

At the very time, then, when Britain ceased to be the world's workshop, she transformed herself into its shipper, banker and insurance agent.

FURTHER READING

W. T. Jackman, *The Development of Transportation in Modern England* (London, Cass, 1962) contains a vast amount of factual material but is too unwieldly to be of use except for reference purposes.

C. I. Savage, *An Economic History of Transport* (London, Hutchinson, 1966) is much more manageable.

C. Hadfield, *British Canals* (Newton Abbot, David and Charles, 1969) and *The Canal Age* (Newton Abbot, David and Charles, 1968) consider canals.

J. Simmons, *The Railways of Britain* (London, Routledge, 1965), M. Robbins, *The Railway Age* (Harmondsworth, Penguin, 1965) and H. Perkin, *The Age of the Railway* (London, Panther, 1970) consider railways.

L. T. C. Rolt, *George and Robert Stephenson* (London, Longmans, 1960) and *Isambard Kingdom Brunel* (Harmondsworth, Penguin, 1970) are both spendid biographies.

Chapter 7

OVERSEAS TRADE AND FOREIGN INVESTMENT

TRADE AND THE INDUSTRIAL REVOLUTION

It is impossible to make an accurate quantitative evaluation of the contribution of overseas trade to the process of industrialisation, but certainly, expanding export markets helped to generate business optimism and stimulate capital investment, in new technologies of production, particularly in the key industry, cotton, which presents a classic example of 'export-led growth'.

The expansion of overseas trade in the eighteenth century was based on the following factors:

1. Rising population in established colonies, such as America and Ireland, meant an enlarged capacity to absorb British manufactures and supply raw materials (especially cotton and flax) and food (grain) in return.
2. The acquisition, largely by war, of new colonies – Canada, India, West Indies – enabled Britain to enlarge her markets still further and draw on supplies of new trade goods, e.g. furs and timber from Canada.
3. The re-export trade to Europe began to grow rapidly: goods from the Empire (particularly cod, sugar, tobacco, rum, molasses, indigo, rice) were brought to Britain, processed (e.g. sugar-refining) and then re-exported to Europe. By the end of the century re-exports accounted for one-third of all exports, a great boost to the balance of payments.

Cotton played a leading part in the second great wave of export expansion (the 1780s; the first was the 1730s and 1740s). For the first time, Britain had a bulk export for tropical and semi-tropical markets (woollen textiles had been unsaleable and trade with these areas had been financed by an outflow of specie). It is important to note that the raw material for this growth industry was *wholly* imported, a fact which draws attention to the mutual relationship between the expansion of domestic and overseas markets. Britain's colonies could never have paid for British manufactured goods if Britain had not generated Colonial incomes by her willingness to absorb colonial goods. Economic growth is a dynamic process which acknowledges no frontiers.

THE FRENCH WARS

From 1793 to 1815 trading conditions were disturbed by war. Napoleon's Continental System, based on the Berlin and Milan decrees of 1806 and 1807, was intended to bring Britain to her knees by blockading the Continent against British goods. He aimed to promote disorder in Britain by denying British manufacturers their most profitable outlet. The result, he hoped, would be unemployment, riots, the collapse of the war-time paper currency, the fall of the government and a French invasion to 'liberate' the oppressed. In fact, Napoleon's control of the European coastline was too incomplete to make his strategy a success. Goods were smuggled in via Sicily, the Azores, Gothenburg or Heligoland and restrictions were periodically lifted to enable French farmers to sell their grain or army contractors to buy great-coats from Leeds! In a sense, the Continental system was a positive benefit as it obliged British traders to search out new markets in South America (where the Spanish colonies began to seize their independence) and India (where the East India Company lost its monopoly in 1813). Britain's retaliatory 'Orders-in-Council', however, did lead to war against the United States (1812–14) which seriously, if temporarily, dislocated trading relations between the two countries.

THE ADVENT OF FREE TRADE

British merchants, accustomed to naval protection and government assistance, were hesitant in their response to the opportunities of peace-time. Contrary to traditional belief, they had to be cajoled into accepting Free Trade by an enlightened and progressive Board of Trade rather than vice versa. Tooke's famous 'Petition' of 1820 was not representative of general mercantile opinion, and, indeed, he had some difficulty in enlisting signatories. Nor could it be said that British traders felt confident that the nation's new industrial technology would enable them to undersell all their rivals. Merchants and manufacturers were not the same people and the terms of trade were turning rapidly against Britain as a consequence of her rapidly rising productivity. By 1860 it was necessary to sell twice as much as it had been in 1800 to get the same amount of imports in return.

Huskisson started the movement towards freer trade in the 1820s, when, as President of the Board of Trade, he abolished embargoes and prohibitive duties, extended the system of imperial preferences, and initiated a general rationalisation of tariffs. The real turning-points were Peel's great Budgets of 1842–5 whereby tariffs were drastically lowered and income-tax reintroduced to provide the government with a bridging revenue during the transitional period in which trade was expected to expand unrestricted and eventually bring in the old volume of revenue from a minimal scale of charges, whose sole purpose was to raise revenue rather than to protect, distort or discriminate against the product of various industries. It was a daring policy which the country accepted against the background of chaos in the nation's finances (the Whigs were defeated at the 1841 election, having run out of reforming steam and having involved the nation in disastrous and wasteful wars against China and Afghanistan) and the worst depression of the century. In such circumstances Britain was prepared to accept a fundamentally new policy which aimed to restore the government's solvency and the nation's prosperity.

The repeal of the Corn Laws (1846) and of the Navigation Laws (1849), Gladstone's tariff-reductions (1853–60) and the Cobden–Chevalier treaty (1860) completed Peel's work and coincided with a vast expansion of exports.

After half a century of stagnant values, exports leaped from *c.* £40,000,000 in 1840 to *c.* £240,000,000 in 1875. Many contemporaries regarded this as the reward of Providence for the pursuit of a courageous and enlightened policy of *laissez-faire*. Others, more perceptive, gave credit to the stimuli of railway construction, general population expansion, the widespread adoption of factory techniques, and the constant improvement in communications effected by the telegraph (Channel cable laid 1851, Atlantic cable 1866), the steamship and the Suez Canal (1869).

THE EXPORT ECONOMY

At the beginning of the nineteenth century, trade for Britain was a convenience, by the end of the century it was a necessity. As

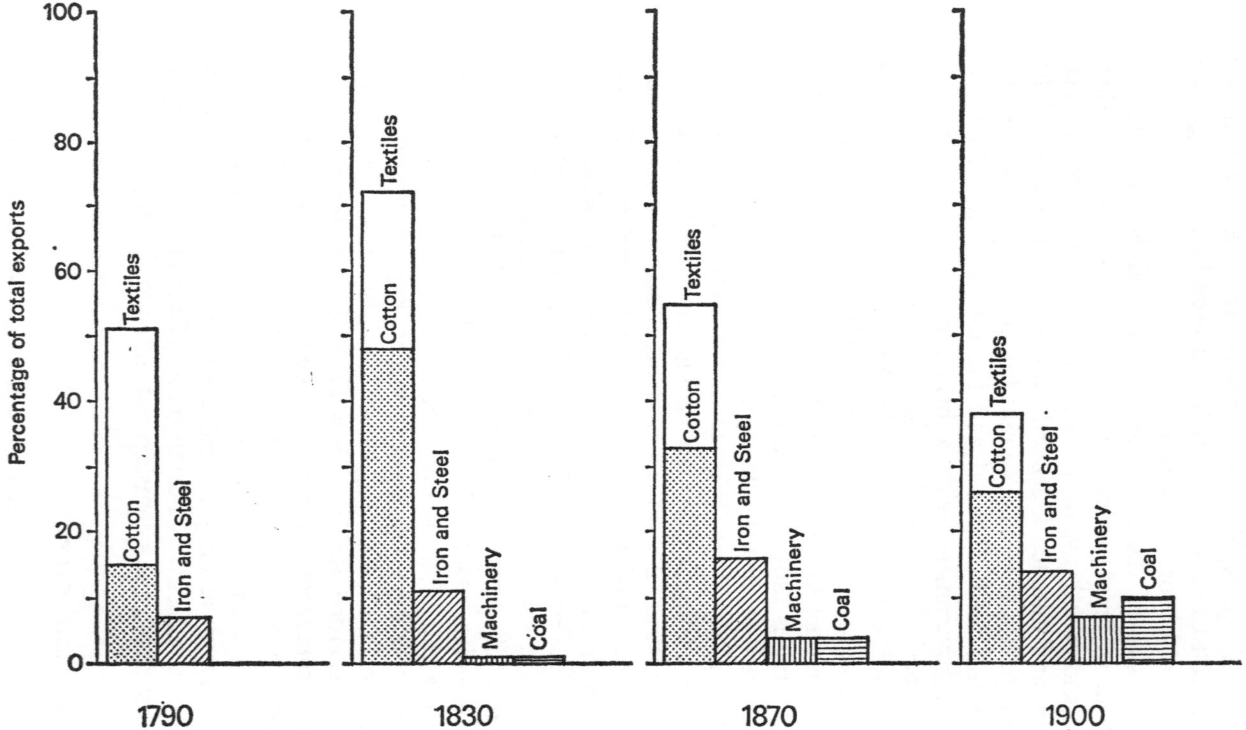

10 Principal Exports, 1740–1909

Note: (i) Textiles includes cotton, woollens, worsteds, silk, linen.

(ii) Iron and steel includes iron, steel, hardware, cutlery, machinery to 1830, thereafter excludes machinery but includes non-ferrous metals.

(iii) To 1830: at 'official values' (i.e. may be regarded as a volume index), thereafter at current prices.

late as the 1820s, the coastal coal trade had exceeded all overseas trade in value. By the end of the century, industry, agriculture and finance were all oriented around overseas trade, and Britain's population, nearly four times what it had been at the time of the first census, was dependent for its livelihood on its ability to sell abroad, and for its daily bread on its ability to import from abroad.

The rapid export expansion of the 1850s and 1860s was checked in the 1870s by the erection of tariff barriers by Russia (1877), France (1878) and Germany (1879). The United States had been pursuing such policies since 1861. The result was stagnation for British exports, at least in terms of values, until the mid-1890s. The *pattern* of trade, however, underwent important changes. Imports diversified to include not only a wider range of foodstuffs (thanks to refrigeration and canning) but also a wider range of manufactured goods – evidence of rising domestic incomes and the technical lead of foreign producers in such fields as the electrical and optical goods industries. Exports were similarly changing as cotton was overshadowed by engineering products and, strangely, a raw material, coal.

The Empire began to play an increasingly prominent role in overseas trade from the 1870s onwards. With Europe and the United States rapidly industrialising behind tariff walls, British manufacturers began to seek out markets in the rapidly developing Empire. India had been a mainstay for cotton since the 1830s; now emigration began to build up Australia, South Africa and Canada, while Great Power rivalries (chiefly the ambitions of Belgium and Germany) precipitated a carve-up of the African interior. The Empire had no tariffs; its pioneer communities needed what Britain could supply (and had previously supplied to the U.S.A.) and, being peopled largely by British emigrants, were eager to buy the British consumer goods they had long been familiar with. Nothing could be more symbolic of the changed attitude to the Empire than Disraeli's conversion to its cause. In his youth he had referred to the colonies as 'millstones round our necks'. In 1874 he named the maintenance of imperial interests as one of the three cardinal policies of the Conservative Party, and in 1877 he made Victoria Empress of India. Of course, there was more to imperialism than a search for new markets or a change of heart on the part of the government. Missionary activity, 'jingoism', the individual enterprise of men like Cecil

Rhodes, all played their part as well. And attachment to the Empire by no means eclipsed attachment to Free Trade. Joseph Chamberlain's attempt to persuade the nation to meet European tariffs by 'Fair Trade' within an enclosed, multilateral imperial trading enclave, was decisively rejected by the electorate.

THE BALANCE OF PAYMENTS

From 1815 onwards Britain's balance of merchandise trade was unfavourable. Despite the flood of textiles, hardware, iron rails and miscellaneous manufactures which was poured out by her enlarged industrial sector, she was unable to produce enough to pay for the rising import bill. All raw cotton was imported as well as (increasingly) the bulk of timber, wool and a growing range of foodstuffs. The trade gap was sealed by invisible exports, which more than compensated for the deficit in visible trade and left a healthy surplus for foreign investment. These invisible earnings were largely generated from two sources – foreign investment (see next section) and a complex of interlocking service industries based on Britain's massive two-way trade with the world – namely shipping, insurance and merchant banking. As the century wore on, and particularly after the 1870s and the loss of industrial supremacy, these service industries came to dominate the nation's prosperity, its financial institutions and its economic thinking. Dependent for growth on the continued expansion of world trade, it was the shipping, financial and commercial interests which defended classic free trade doctrine against the questionings of steel-producers or agriculturalists. In this period, these City interests, supported by the trading strength of the pound sterling, made London the hub of the international multilateral trade system. International trade meant very largely trade with Britain and almost certainly trade *through* Britain. As Professor Mathias has observed,

> . . . in the new foreign markets being created by British merchants. India, South-East Asia, Australia, Africa, South America, China, most of the enterprise behind the trade, both ways, was British. These countries did not have long-distance merchant shipping fleets of their own, no local discount markets, no powerful insurance brokers, often few indigenous merchant houses who would keep in non-British hands the profits of

internal distribution of British exports inland to final customers (*The First Industrial Nation*).

This process was assisted not only by the extension and improvement of communications by railways and steamships, but also by the electric telegraph, which enabled shipowners to maintain contact with fleets of wandering 'tramps', directing them from port to port in search of cargo. By thus diminishing periods of enforced idleness, the telegraph helped raise the productivity of the shipping industry. It also gave birth to a new form of international trade, as Professor W. M. Stern has noted:

> Once news of the quantity and quality of a distant harvest could travel faster than the crop itself, merchants could buy it unseen for later delivery. Markets in 'futures' grew up, in which men bought and sold produce yet to come. This enabled manufacturers to cover requirements of raw materials for a period ahead at a firm price which could be embodied in cost calculations (*Britain, Yesterday and Today*).

The Balance of Payments of the United Kingdom, 1816–1913

Annual averages in £m. All figures have been rounded

	(1) Balance of visible trade	(2) Net shipping earnings	(3) Profits, interest, dividends	(4) Insurance, brokerage, commissions	(5) Emigrants, tourists, smugglers, government, all other	(6) Balance of invisible trade	(7) Net balance
1816–20	−11	+10	+ 8	+3	−3	+18	+ 7
1821–25	− 8	+ 9	+ 9	+2	−2	+18	+10
1826–30	−15	+ 8	+ 9	+2	−3	+17	+ 3
1831–35	−13	+ 5	+11	+3	−4	+19	+ 6
1836–40	−23	+11	+15	+4	−4	+26	+ 3
1841–45	−19	+12	+15	+4	−5	+25	+ 6
1846–50	−26	+14	+18	+4	−6	+30	+ 5
1851–55	−33	+19	+24	+6	−8	+41	+ 8
1856–60	−34	+26	+33	+8	−8	+60	+26
1861–65	−59	+34	+44	+11	−8	+81	+22
1866–70	−65	+45	+57	+13	−9	+106	+41
1871–75	−64	+51	+83	+16	−12	+139	+75
1876–80	−124	+54	+88	+16	− 9	+149	+25
1881–85	− 99	+60	+96	+16	−11	+161	+61
1886–90	− 89	+57	+115	+15	−11	+177	+88
1891–95	−134	+57	+124	+15	−10	+186	+52
1896–1900	−159	+62	+132	+16	−11	+199	+40
1901–05	−177	+71	+149	+18	−13	+226	+49
1906–10	−144	+89	+196	+22	−18	+290	+146
1911–13	−140	+100	+241	+27	−22	+346	+206

Source: Imlah, *Economic Elements of the Pax Britannica* (Cambridge, Mass., 1958), pp. 70–75

FOREIGN INVESTMENT

During the French wars, London became the world's financial capital, almost by default. Amsterdam had formerly dominated the international money market, but the stagnation of the Dutch economy in the eighteenth century had weakened its hold. The French invasion of the Netherlands demonstrated its strategic vulnerability. London, of necessity, became Europe's deposit-box. There was nowhere else – Paris was the capital of a revolutionary republic, Berlin of an agrarian despotism; St Petersburg and New York were small and far away. London was safe from invasion and at the cross-roads of the international trade routes. Under the impetus of foreign capital seeking safety and foreign governments seeking loans, London's financial mechanism began to grow in size and sophistication.

The war-time expansion of the National Debt and the unequal division of the growing National Income created a *rentier*-class of stockholders eager to find profitable outlets for their surplus wealth. Agriculture in the post-war period was an unattractive proposition; industry was self-financing. It was an age of comfortable living, but not of conspicuous consumption. Waste in riotous living or aesthetic self-indulgence seemed less desirable than the high interest rates offered by foreign borrowers. Europe was the breeding-ground for confidence. France borrowed £10,000,000 to finance her war indemnity. Prussia (£5,000,000), Russia (£2,000,000) and Austria (£1,000,000), borrowed to keep liberalism at bay. In the 1820s South America beckoned a golden finger and some £24,000,000 was raised to finance mining ventures and new governments. The latter proved as unrewarding as the former, and there was a general collapse in 1825.

The flow was resumed in the 1830s, this time to the United States where the boom in Anglo-American trade (which doubled between 1830 and 1836) led to a wave of investment in canals, roads, and banks. President Jackson's Specie Circular, requiring payments for public lands to be made in hard money rather than paper, checked the bonanza in 1836. The collapse came in 1839 when numerous banks crashed and a number of state governments defaulted as the whole American monetary system endured a general crisis of confidence.

Railways carried foreign investment through the 1840s as France, Belgium and Prussia began to imitate England's example with Scottish engineers, Welsh iron, Irish labour and English capital. The revolutions of 1848 showed how railways could be used to deploy troops quickly, and gave a boost to construction in Austria and Italy. In the 1850s India was the main new source of demand, again for railway finance, and the Mutiny of 1857 did for the sub-continent's strategic thinking what 1848 had done for Europe's. The American Civil War (1861–5) and the Austro-Prussian War (1866) again demonstrated the military value of railways and led to new waves of borrowing, while the completion of the Suez Canal (1869) drew Egypt's luckless rulers into the coils of the international money market. In 1850 British foreign investments had totalled about £200,000,000, realising an annual income of £12,000,000. Between 1870 and 1875 the outflow had reached a peak of £75,000,000 per annum, well in excess of yearly earnings from previous investments, which now amounted to £1,000,000,000 and brought in an annual £50,000,000. Thereafter, the investment process was more or less self-sustaining as dividends from successful ventures were ploughed back into new schemes rather than repatriated. The establishment of stable government in Argentina (1865) led to the rapid development of the Pampas by British capital. In 1875 total British investment in Argentina was a mere £2,000,000; ten years later it was £45,000,000 and by 1890, £175,000,000. South African mines dominated the 1890s; Australia and Canada were the main targets for the last great speculative wave of 1910–13.

On the eve of the Great War, British foreign investments totalled over £4,000,000,000. Half was in the Empire – and three-quarters of that in the white Dominions. Europe, where the whole process had begun, accounted for only one-twelfth. America was still the largest single foreign debtor, holding one-quarter. Of the rest, most was in South America, the Middle and the Far East. More than two-fifths was in railways; the remainder being in mines, plantations, public utilities and government stocks. Almost none was in industry.

The effects of foreign investment on Great Britain were as follows:

1. It opened up new areas of supply (e.g. Argentina: beef, grain and hides) and created the means for its own repayment (railways made of British iron) which promoted a return flow of British goods.

2. It enabled the balance of payments to remain 'in the black'. Foreign investment earnings alone would have been enough to cover the merchandise deficit. As income from other 'invisibles' (notably shipping) was sufficient for this purpose, investment earnings were used to maintain the flow of funds abroad.

3. It could be argued that foreign investment, by opening up new markets for old goods, and cushioning the balance of payments, enabled Britain to evade the problem of restructuring the export industries to meet the challenge of foreign industrial competition.

4. It has also been argued that the funds absorbed by foreign investment could have been more usefully employed at home, e.g.

(i) by improving housing and public health services – but there would not have been the large-scale imports of cheap food which did so much to raise living standards after the 1870s;

(ii) by re-equipping industry – but there is no evidence that it was 'starved' of capital. In 1913 7.5 per cent of the National Income went to foreign investment and only 4.5 per cent of domestic capital formation. But this only reflected the unwillingness of British entrepreneurs to contemplate change and bid up interest rates until they became attractive enough to lenders.

As D. H. Aldcroft and H. W. Richardson have concluded:

> The benefits to the lender, both from a national and the investor's points of view, were beyond doubt before 1914. Although some investors lost large sums, especially when they had invested in unstable European, Middle Eastern or Latin American governments, defaults were relatively rare. The average rate of return, varying between 4½ per cent and 6 per cent over the 1870–1914 period as a whole . . . was rather higher than on domestic loans. It is impossible to quantify the national benefits, but they were substantial (*The British Economy, 1870–1939*).

FURTHER READING

W. E. Minchinton, *The Growth of English Overseas Trade in the Seventeenth and Eighteenth Centuries* (London, Methuen, 1969: Debates in Economic History series) brings together half a dozen articles on this subject.

S. B. Saul, *Studies in British Overseas Trade, 1870–1914* (Liverpool University Press, 1960) is rather technical.

P. Deane, *The First Industrial Revolution* (Cambridge University Press, 1965), P. Mathias, *The First Industrial Nation, 1700–1914* (London, Methuen, 1969) and S. G. Checkland, *The Rise of the Industrial Society in England, 1815–85* (London, Longmans, 1964) deal quite adequately with the subject, and W. Ashworth, *An Economic History of England 1870–1939* (Methuen, 1960) contains much numerical data. All have excellent bibliographies on the subject.

L. H. Jenks, *The Migration of British Capital to 1875* (London, Nelson, 1963) deals very readably with foreign investment.

A. R. Hall (ed.), *The Export of Capital from Britain, 1870–1914* (London, Methuen, 1968) collects together much up-to-date research on this subject.

Chapter 8

LIFE AND LABOUR

STANDARDS OF LIVING

The Early Nineteenth Century – The Debate

How far did the Industrial Revolution benefit the working man? Historians today disagree almost as much as those who lived through the period. Among the earliest economic historians, the socialist Hammonds, following the evidence of such writers as Engels and Marx, saw industrialisation as an almost unmitigated disaster for the mass of British men and women, involving them in complete social disruption without affording them the compensation of higher material standards of living. A later generation of revisionists, notably Sir John Clapham and T. S. Ashton, have cast doubt on the value of generalised contemporary polemics, whether they be those of Engels or Cobbett, as valid evidence for changes in material standards. In the last decade or so, the debate has been renewed with vigour by scholars armed with novel statistical techniques and methods drawn largely from the social sciences.

When specialists disagree, the ordinary student must tread warily, learn to avoid specious arguments and try, at least, to learn *why* the specialists disagree. Largely, the problem for this period (*c.* 1790–*c.* 1840) is one of evidence:

1. There are no accurate figures for such key items of ordinary budgets as rent and fuel.
2. Figures of wage-rates are readily available, but are usually for particular areas, industries and years. Long series are lacking and, most important of all, we cannot know what adjustments to make for such factors as overtime, unemployment and payments in kind.
3. The price of various goods is often known, but changes in quality may go undetected. Many price series are misleading

because they are based on data drawn from institutions such as schools or hospitals which purchased on special contract terms.

4. It is also necessary to be clear whether any particular set of statistics is for England and Wales, Great Britain or the United Kingdom. The inclusion of Ireland makes a great deal of difference: according to the French writer de Tocqueville, its people were the poorest in Europe in the 1840s and, numbering some 8.5 million, they accounted for one-third of the population of the U.K.

5. As ever, the historian must beware of 'averages' which conceal crucial differences, and stereotypes, like 'the ordinary working man', which take no account of the particularities of occupation, region, age and size of family. Nor may the psychological perspective be ignored. Even if noise, smoke and dirt form no part of the economists' unsubtle calculation of living standards, it is as well to remember the effects wrought by migration, redundancy and environmental horrors. Finally the following comment by E. J. Hobsbawm, Marxist leader of the current school of pessimists, must be borne in mind:

> There is, of course, no dispute about the fact that relatively the poor grew poorer, simply because the country and its rich and middle class grew wealthier. The very moment when the poor were at the end of their tether – in the early and middle forties – was the moment when the middle classes dripped with excess capital, to be wildly invested in railways and spent on the bulging, opulent household furnishings displayed at the Great Exhibition of 1851 (*Industry and Empire*).

On balance the conclusion seems to be that living standards did not change much either way, and, if anything, they deteriorated. The period 1790–1815 was almost certainly one of deterioration, the post-war years were difficult for many, the twenties prosperous, the thirties stagnant, and the early forties almost universally catastrophic. That the period was not one of definite and far-reaching deterioration in living standards was, in the view of Professor Mathias, something of a triumph for the maturing economy, given the scale of investment in these years and the rapid expansion of population, especially (non-productive) children.

The early nineteenth century. There are various arguments for and against a rise in the standard of living in the early nineteenth century, but as so much of the statistical evidence is suspect and can be competently debated only by experts, the arguments that will be considered here are more general and *a priori*.

The case in favour of a rise, however slight, in standards of living rests on the following main points:

1. The new steam-powered, mechanised technology of production lowered costs dramatically and brought cheap cottons, hardware, pottery, etc., within the purchasing range of the labouring poor.

2. Transport improvements contributed substantially to lowering the prices of basic items like food and fuel, as well as manufactured goods. (Prices certainly did fall overall.)

3. Industrialisation required new skills, created new employment opportunities and raised wages by upgrading jobs.

4. Expanding trade widened the range of imported goods available to consumers.

5. There is clear evidence that skilled workers were generally better off, except when new technologies made them redundant.

The case against a rise seems more convincing:

1. Population was rising rapidly and large numbers of women, children and Irish were flooding on to the labour market. Unions were treated with hostility by employers and government alike, while many workers regarded them with indifference. The result was that labour had a poor bargaining position *vis-à-vis* capital, and had little chance of improving it.

2. The inflation of the Napoleonic wars clearly benefited farmers, manufacturers with government contracts, and *rentiers* with government stocks. During the quarter century after the war, servicing of the enormous National Debt required heavy taxes on articles of common consumption (tea, sugar, soap) to provide an annual transfer of incomes from the poor to the rich (fundholders) of about £30,000,000.

3. Housing was in very short supply and building-materials were taxed; thus rents must have risen as population increased and moved into towns.

4. The chief beneficiaries of steam technology were Britain's foreign customers – now able to buy manufactures much cheaper. (The terms of trade turned heavily against Britain in this period.)

5. A number of large groups can be shown to have endured significant deterioration: handloom weavers (250,000 in 1833),

squeezed out by the power loom in the 1830s and early 1840s; agricultural workers (about a million), depressed by Speenhamland; casual labourers (hundreds of thousands), the first casualties of every depression.

6. There were numerous severe outbreaks of social discontent: 1811–13 (Luddites), 1815–17 and 1819 (Radicals), 1830 (agricultural labourers under 'Captain Swing'), 1831–2 (in favour of Parliamentary reform, supported by the masses as a social panacea), 1835–6 (against the New Poor Law), 1839–42 and 1848 (Chartists and Anti-Corn Law Leaguers: Rebecca Riots directed against turnpikes in Wales). Most of these took place in years of high bread prices and unemployment. There were many other minor local outbreaks (e.g. bread riots in East Anglia 1816 and 1822), and overall there was a 'sense of imminent social explosion' (E. J. Hobsbawm).

7. It was pre-eminently an 'age of investment', with the rising National Income being absorbed into factories, machines, buildings, docks and railways, rather than diverted into the bellies and pockets of the poor. As E. P. Thompson has observed, all that the poor man got out of the first phase of industrial growth was some cheap cotton, a few cheap candles and a great number of articles in the *Economic History Review*!

The Great Victorian Boom

There can be little doubt that in the thirty years or so of the central Victorian period, living standards for the majority of Englishmen began to rise. The growth of railways contributed materially to increasing the mobility of labour (particularly away from overpopulated rural areas) and led directly to the expansion of employment in heavy industry (metals, coal, engineering), which had reverberating multiplier and accelerator effects throughout the whole economy. As world markets expanded, profits soared and employers, no longer so terrified of bankruptcy or shortage of capital, could afford to be more generous in wage settlements.

Other factors, beside general economic expansion, played their part. Trade unions won *de facto* and later *de jure* recognition. Although they only covered a small percentage of the labour force, they began to set the pace in forcing up wages. Co-operative societies multiplied, bringing cheaper, and, more important, unadulterated goods to the working man's wife. The truck shops, which they set out to combat, dwindled away. Legislation, too, played its part. Factory Acts improved working conditions and, by regulating hours, took the competitive edge off women and children's labour. Public health legislation began, slowly, to improve the environment and diminish the threat of epidemic disease. From 1871 Bank Holidays became general public holidays.

It was the workers in industry (and they were well under half of the labour force) who benefited most in this period, especially in boom sectors like iron-founding. But even they could be reduced to desperate straits by sudden slumps like that of 1857, or protracted crises like the Lancashire 'cotton famine' of the 1860s. Moreover, at a time when they were responsible for their own social security through savings-clubs and Friendly Societies like the Foresters and the Oddfellows, they were peculiarly liable to cyclical unemployment and as vulnerable as any other sector to industrial injury.

Agricultural workers, on the other hand, did not share in the general prosperity. Paradoxically, it required a depression in agriculture to raise their condition. Casual workers, dockers and workers in the 'sweated' industries (like tailoring or box-making) seem to have fared no better. Naturally it was the capitalist employing class which came off best, thrifty as ever, but now with a surplus for neo-Gothic suburban villas, seaside and Continental holidays and public school education for their sons. The instant publishing success of Mrs Beeton's famous and monumental *Book of Household Management* (1859) says all that needs to be said.

The Great Depression

In this period (1873–96) living standards took their greatest and most sustained step forward. There is plenty of evidence:

1. The rising consumption of such foodstuffs as beer (which reached a peak of consumption in 1899), sugar (1860, 35 lbs per head per year, 1910, 85 lbs), and meat (consumption rose by one-third) show that the pattern of the working-man's diet was definitely changing. Cheap carbohydrate fillers were giving way to increased intakes of protein in the form of meat, cheese and fish. Chocolate, jam and biscuits, roller-ground white flour and condensed milk helped henceforth to sweeten, and rot, the tooth of the worker and his offspring.

2. New patterns of expenditure extended to 'consumer durables' like bicycles (Blatchford's Clarion Clubs made it a national craze), musical instruments (a drawing-room piano was the ultimate status symbol), and sewing-machines (a girl's best friend, in the words of a popular song). These, like a gold watch-and-chain, were for the skilled artisan and his family, but nearly all regular wage-earners could now share in the delights of ready-made clothes and factory-made boots, the fish-and-chip shop, the music-hall, the seaside excursion and mass spectator sports (professionalism in soccer was recognised in 1885). Trams (average fare 1½*d.*)

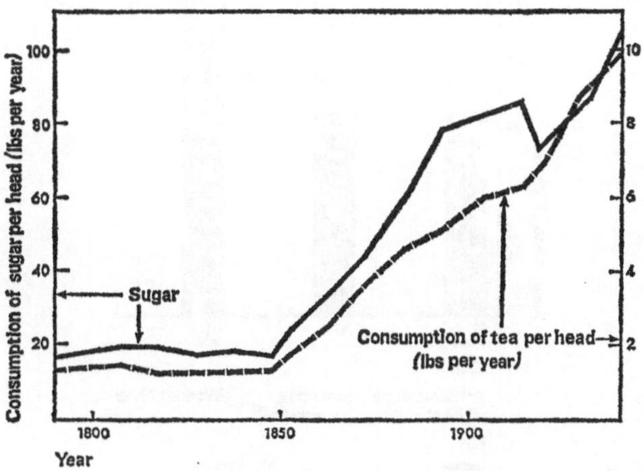

11 Consumption of Tea and Sugar

meant more to the working man than railways ever had, despite 'Workmen's Fares' becoming general in 1883. Newspapers, like the sensational *Pall Mall Gazette*, with its novel headlines, and the tabloid *Daily Mail* (1895), reflected rising standards of literacy, while the mushroom growth of retail multiples, under such giants as Lipton, Sainsbury, Boot and Burton, reflected the growth of a mass market for the necessities of everyday life, though it was, of course, the perfection of the railway system which permitted the centralised control and supplying of Britain's 2,000 chain butchers, 2,600 shoe-shops and 3,500 grocers by 1900.

3. Housing standards remained low, though regulation of building had started and the worst of the old 'back-to-backs' were beginning to be demolished. Clean water-supplies and gas for

lighting, heating and cooking, were more generally available. The average span of life was increasing, but infant mortality, that most sensitive indicator of social conditions, remained as high as ever.

What caused this remarkable improvement in the nation's condition? A combination of the following factors:

1. The Reform Acts of 1867 and 1884 had given most men the vote, which made their material well-being a matter of political concern, whatever *laissez-faire* decreed.

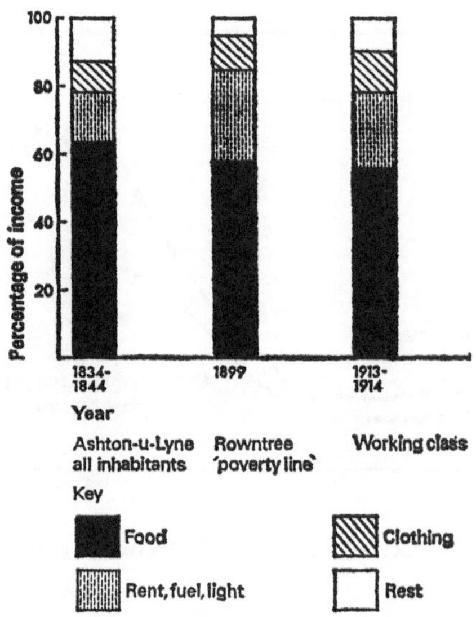

12 Family Expenditure of Workers

2. The bargaining position of labour was strengthened by the firm legal position of the trade unions after 1875 and the high rate of emigration, which drew much labour off the market. The spread of education after 1870 helped to cut out children's labour.

3. Industrialisation was reaching a new stage of maturity. Large plants with complex, expensive machinery were becoming general in the manufacturing industry, and employers, who now required sobriety, literacy and initiative, rather than brute force and sullen obedience, began to see how higher wages could create incentives and improve the quality of labour. Upgrading of skills,

and the creation of a new class of semi-skilled workers was itself a consequence of this process.

4. Social services, however niggardly, began to add indirectly to incomes – education, health regulations, municipal baths and wash-houses, and, after a long battle, legal compensation for men injured at work, whether through the employer's negligence or not, was introduced.

5. The greatest importance must, however, be attached to the importation of cheap food, if only because it represented so high a proportion of *every* working man's expenditure. Railways and refrigerated steam-ships now brought wheat from the U.S.A., 'bully beef' from Argentina and lamb from New Zealand. At the same time, canning extended the range of available fruits.

Edwardian England

The years from 1896 to 1914 were an Indian summer for British capitalism. Profits recovered, investment went abroad with renewed confidence, prices turned upward once again. Real wages, however, stagnated or fell slightly as money wages failed to keep pace. A new bitterness entered industrial relations and the unions, growing rapidly in spite of the times, won important victories in the Coal Mines Regulation Act (1908), which gave the pitmen an eight-hour day (at the coal-face, walking there could take an hour or more each way), and the Shops Act (1912), which gave assistants a half day off. School meals (1906) and medical inspection (1907), old-age pensions (1908) and National Insurance (1911) all helped, and the workers in the 'sweated' industries were given minimum wages by the Trade Boards Act (1909).

Despite these measures, and despite the real advances of the 'Great Depression' period, poverty continued to plague the nation. Seebohm Rowntree's *Poverty: A Study of Town Life* was based on a scientific survey of conditions in York. It showed that 27 per cent of the population were living in 'primary poverty', that is their incomes were insufficient to maintain mere physical efficiency. The Boer War recruiting figures, published as a shock report in 1904, were alarming to those whose consciences were touched by strategic rather than humanitarian considerations – after a century and a half of undoubted economic progress, one-third of the nation's manhood was medically certified as incapable of military service.

LABOUR ORGANISATION

The transformation wrought by the Industrial Revolution was social as much as economic – old ways of life were erased, communities uprooted and created. The fear of redundancy hung over the working population, who were obliged to accept a new and harsher work discipline in which the employer acknowledged no paternal obligation towards his faceless, dehumanised 'hands'. As Marx and Engels so vehemently put it:

> The bourgeoisie . . . has put an end to all feudal, patriarchal, idyllic relations. It has pitilessly torn asunder the motley feudal ties that bound man to his 'natural superiors' and has left remaining no other nexus between man and man but naked self-interest, than callous 'cash-payment'. . . . In one word, for exploitation, veiled by religious and political illusions, it has substituted naked, shameless, direct, brutal exploitation (*The Communist Manifesto*).

The reactions of the masses were as diverse as the experiences they endured.

Violent rejection was common enough in the eighteenth century, particularly when a bad harvest raised the price of bread and diminished the opportunities for harvest employment. 'Bread-riots' continued to occur, but a newer form of protest, machine-smashing, was more symptomatic of the times. The Luddites smashed stocking-frames in Nottinghamshire in 1811; agricultural labourers smashed threshing machines in the South in the 1820s.

Some hoped for amelioration of their condition through legislation, and supported the mass agitations for Parliamentary reform in 1815–19 and 1830–2. Excluded from the franchise by the Reform Act (1832), they turned to Chartism, particularly during the depression years of 1839–42. Its programme was vague enough to have wide appeal – a thorough reform of Parliament as laid out by the six points of the 'People's Charter' (universal male suffrage, secret ballot, annual elections, equal electoral areas, abolition of property qualification for M.P.s, payment of M.P.s), followed by a general reform of British institutions by legislative decree. Compounded with this strategy was Feargus O'Connor's anachronistic 'Land Plan', a scheme to turn industrial Britain into a rural utopia of peasant cultivators. The fact that it won such widespread popular support reveals how deeply the masses rejected the values of the new order, even as late as the 1840s.

The number of people actively engaged in political movements was very small. For most, such involvement was sporadic and momentary. Drink, cruel sports or revivalist religion probably attracted larger and more permanent bodies of adherents. The response which had the most important long-term effects was the urge to form combinations among workers with a view to improving their wages and conditions of employment. The modern trade union movement is the product of nearly two centuries of industrial struggle, the main outlines of which will be sketched below.

Trade Unionism

To 1850. The Early Development

During the late eighteenth and early nineteenth centuries, the unions were extremely active, but ephemeral and largely ineffective. Most were localised in their membership and horizons, springing up in prosperous times to be wiped out by the next depression. Some were formed *ad hoc* to oppose a cut in wages or win a rise, and then disbanded when the struggle was over, whatever the outcome. The idea of a union as a permanent body with a national membership and a defined strategy, was to emerge only slowly.

The chief restraints on the development of effective unionism in this period were:

1. The rapid increase in population and its dilution by women, children and immigrants put labour in a weak bargaining position.

2. The attitude of the government was one of hostility, particularly during and shortly after the French wars, when any 'combination' might be labelled a conspiracy with revolutionary intentions. The Combination Laws (1799–1800 – repealed 1824) were less severe than is generally believed. Three months' imprisonment was almost a free pardon compared with the savage penalties of death or transportation inflicted for petty thefts. Many trade societies, moreover, continued to operate openly and successfully throughout the period in which the laws were in existence. Even after their repeal, though, the government, which had left unions in a legal limbo of being neither legal nor illegal, could penalise their members by prosecutions for conspiracy or administering unlawful oaths, as in the celebrated case of the Tolpuddle martyrs (1834).

3. Employers were also hostile to unions as they believed that if they paid higher wages, they would have less profits to finance further expansion (an argument which held good only for the very short run). They often refused to acknowledge the existence of unions, or negotiate with their leaders. Strike-breaking was also easy for them in a period of labour-surplus.

4. Unions had difficulty in finding leaders, particularly at the local level. The great figures of the movement, like Robert Owen, were often visionaries or revolutionaries, desiring to replace industrial capitalism rather than to accept its framework and better the condition of the working man within it. At the local level, unions were hampered by the lack of men with sufficient literacy, self-confidence and social status to be taken seriously by employers and workers alike. The mere routine business of correspondence and subscriptions could defeat an unlettered artisan. Many potential leaders were also diverted by the appeals of Parliamentary reform, Chartism, opposition to the new Poor Law, or agitation for the Factory Acts.

The only really successful unions in this period were the craft unions, which had long existed to protect the interests of skilled men such as printers, carpenters, shipwrights, etc. They had a marketable commodity to offer, their skill, and the high wages they received enabled them to build up an effective strike fund, and impose conditions on their employers. The enforcement of apprenticeship regulations enabled them to limit the number of new recruits to the craft and keep wage levels up. They considered themselves (and rightly so) vastly better off than the mass of depressed labourers, with whom they had no common interests. Thus the 'aristocracy of labour', which might have provided the cadres to make mass unionism a reality, concentrated their efforts on maintaining the gap between themselves and the bulk of the working population.

1851–75. The Period of Consolidation

This was the period of the New Model Unions, of which the Amalgamated Society of Engineers was the first. They were craft unions, with high dues (one shilling per week) and a cautious policy of striking only when there were no alternatives and when they were sure of victory. For the most part, they used their funds to provide members with their own system of social security, paying out benefits in case of sickness, bereavement or unemployment. United in the 'Junta' they consolidated the legal position of the trade union movement during a difficult period. The public outcry at the 'Sheffield Outrages' (1866) in which cutlers had brutally assaulted non-union men, the *Hornby* v. *Close* (1867) decision, which denied the legal existence of unions and thus their capacity to protect funds against embezzlement, and the initial hostility of a Royal Commission on Trade Unions (1867) were all reversed by the patient, skilful moderation of the movement's leadership (who were beginning to think of themselves as a *movement* – the T.U.C. was founded in 1868). The Trade Union Act (1871) and the Conspiracy and Protection of Property Act (1875) gave unions, (many of whose members could now use a vote to their advantage) legal existence and the right to strike and picket.

By 1872 about a million men belonged to trade unions. The expansion of their membership over the previous quarter century can be regarded as the indirect consequence of the expansion of the heavy industry sector of the economy. More men were concentrated in large units with common grievances; more men had a skill to sell and a lifelong commitment to one trade, which they were willing to defend by striking. But this enlarged membership represented only a fraction of those even in manufacturing industry. Joseph Arch's agricultural unions foundered after a few years and the service industries (transport, retailing, domestic service) were still quite untouched.

1880–1914. The Period of Growth

The continued expansion of trade union membership during this period can be attributed to the following developments:

1. The extension of large plant production throughout industry created more large units and led to an upgrading of skills.

2. Rising incomes, growing literacy, the Reform Acts of 1867 and 1884 and the nascent socialist movement created a new political consciousness among the masses.

3. Continued urbanisation, mass-produced goods and the first 'mass-media' broke down regional differences and moulded the working population into a more socially homogeneous group, able to perceive broad common interests shared by all sections. The growth of a semi-skilled class of operatives, a result of the more

general use of machinery, helped to bridge the former gap between labour aristocrats and the unskilled masses.

4. The vicissitudes of capitalism during the 'Great Depression' of 1873–96, made the property-owning classes less confident of the value of complete *laissez-faire*, while fluctuations in employment (which were borne by such well-organized sections as the shipbuilders and the coal-miners) brought a new bitterness to labour relations.

Membership of Trade Unions and Number of Days Work Lost through Stoppages (thousands), 1893–1914

	Members	Days lost		Members	Days lost
1893	1,559	30,440	1904	1,967	1,460
1894	1,530	9,510	1905	1,997	2,370
1895	1,504	5,700	1906	2,210	3,020
1896	1,608	3,560	1907	2,513	2,150
1897	1,731	10,330	1908	2,485	10,790
1898	1,752	15,260	1909	2,477	2,690
1899	1,911	2,500	1910	2,565	9,870
1900	2,022	3,090	1911	3,139	10,160
1901	2,025	4,130	1912	3,416	40,890
1902	2,013	3,440	1913	4,135	9,800
1903	1,994	2,320	1914	4,145	9,880

A New Unionism emerged with the intention of transcending craft boundaries and embracing all grades of worker into 'general' or 'industry' unions, with nominal subscriptions, minimal security benefits and a policy of militant, aggressive strikes to wring concessions from the employing classes. Notable victories were won by the match-girls (1888), the dockers (1889) and the miners (1908). By the eve of the Great War the union movement could stage national strikes (1911), had twenty-nine 'Labour' M.P.s in Parliament and was forging a powerful Triple Alliance of miners, transport workers and railwaymen (1913), but it still failed to embrace the majority of the labour force.

SELF-HELP

Samuel Smiles's *Self-Help* (1859) was the biggest best-seller of the nineteenth century, outstripping the novels of Dickens and being translated into Turkish, Japanese and Arabic, as well as every major European language. The khedive of Egypt even decorated his palace with inscriptions from what was, in effect, the Holy Writ of industrial capitalism. Its basic argument was simple – any man of *ordinary* talents could, by hard work, thrift and self-improvement, lift himself into a superior station in society. Numerous anecdotes enlivened its pages and reminded the reader of the humble beginnings and great success of such figures as Sir Richard Arkwright, James Brindley, Josiah Wedgwood or George Stephenson. This gospel influenced the lives of millions, and found expression in such characteristic nineteenth-century institutions as the Friendly Society, the Mechanics Institute and the Co-operative Society.

Thrift, the first of Smiles's virtues, was encouraged by Friendly Societies, which were a combination of the poor man's welfare state and bank. Although they had existed in the eighteenth century, 'Orders' such as the Oddfellows and Foresters, and the newly-founded Hearts of Oak (1841) grew mightily as working-class incomes began to rise after the mid-nineteenth century. By 1872 they had 4 million members (most of whom were in Lancashire) and by 1913, 6,500,000. The Post Office Savings Bank (1860) opened another channel in which sixpences and shillings could accumulate into 'respectability'. Temperance societies, by discouraging expenditure on alcohol, indirectly assisted this process.

Self-improvement was fostered by Mechanics Institutes (founded in 1824 by Birkbeck to teach artisans more about their trade and enable them to rise to supervisory positions) by the efforts of the statesman, Brougham, and the publisher, Charles Knight, to diffuse 'Useful Knowledge' by lectures, pamphlets and cheap steam-printed books, by the University Extension scheme (1873), by Ruskin Hall (1899) and the Worker's Educational Association (1903). Trade unions lent their encouragement and financial support.

The Co-operative Movement combined thrift and self-improvement into a collectivist form of 'Self-Help'. Many early socialists, notably Robert Owen, wished to establish communities in which the enormous productivity of industrial capitalism could be used to maximise social welfare by replacing the spirit of competition with the spirit of co-operation. In the event, Co-operatives grew up to unite and protect the interests of men and women as consumers rather than producers. The first was established at Rochdale in 1844 and the ideas it incorporated spread swiftly across the industrial North:

1. Sale of a limited range of sound goods and unadulterated foodstuffs at moderate prices.
2. Honest trading and elimination of the expense of 'middlemen' wherever possible.
3. Redistribution of profits to members as a 'divvy' (dividend) in proportion to the amount they spent. (This could be left in the hands of the society to accumulate as shares, a painless form of saving – thus providing it with funds for further growth.)

In 1863 the North of England Co-operative Wholesale Society was founded (it became the C.W.S. in 1873) to provide goods to the various retail societies. By 1913 it controlled iron-foundries, printing-works, biscuit-, boot- and tobacco-factories and a bank; and the number of 'co-operators' had risen from 546,000 (1881) to 1,700,000 (1900) to 3,000,000 (1913). The 'Co-op' had supported 'self-improvement' by educating its members to be wise consumers, as well as by subsidising lectures, adult-education courses and a Co-operative college.

POVERTY

The problem of the poor became more acute with the onset of industrialisation. Population growth raised their numbers, technology reduced the value of their labour, and the disappearance of by-employments, like spinning and nail-making, together with the decline of whole industrial areas like East Anglia and the West Country, created large rural areas in which surplus labour stagnated for want of employment. Festering social discontent, which occasionally erupted into open disorder, made the problem of poverty a preoccupation of contemporary statesmen, as it had been of their Tudor predecessors, who were similarly concerned that it might lead to revolution and the overthrow of the whole existing structure of society (and neither had tear-gas or riot squads to disperse insurgents without bloodshed).

The Tudors had consolidated their piece-meal attempts to grapple with the problem into a comprehensive statute (1601) which made each parish responsible for its own poor. After the Civil War (1642–9) had smashed the machinery of the royal bureaucracy, poor relief became almost entirely a matter of local initiative, and it was this local initiative which determined the next national policy to emerge.

The years 1793–5 saw a succession of bad harvests; the triumphs of the revolutionary French Republic gave ruling classes everywhere cause for fear. In 1795, at the Pelican Inn, Speenhamland, the Berkshire J.P.s decided to tide over the crisis by paying a dole to wage-earners below a minimum income level, the amount to be calculated according to the price of bread and the size of the recipient's family. The system was widely adopted throughout the agricultural south and east, though not, significantly, in the more industrial north and west. The 'Speenhamland System' became a permanent feature of English rural life for the next forty years; a measure designed to meet a harvest crisis became a palliative for rural overpopulation, with the following consequences:

1. Wages were depressed wherever the system was in force because employers knew that they would be made up to subsistence level out of the rates.
2. Larger families were encouraged, or, at least, not penalised.
3. Labourers were discouraged from moving to seek work for fear of losing their right to relief, which could only be obtained in their parish of 'settlement'.

Thus the Speenhamland System, although it succeeded in keeping the threat of a 'peasants' revolt' at bay, did so by aggravating the basic causes of poverty – rural overpopulation and immobility. The fact that poor rates were constantly rising prompted the reformed Parliament of 1832 to appoint commissioners to look into the matter. Their report, strongly influenced by the Benthamite Edwin Chadwick, led to the Poor Law Amendment Act of 1834, which swept away the Speenhamland System and the principle of 'outdoor relief', except for the 'deserving poor' (aged, blind, orphans). The principles on which relief were henceforth to be given were:

1. Relief was to be given to the able-bodied only if they submitted to the harsh discipline of the workhouse (with uniforms, no smoking, separation of the sexes, etc.).
2. Conditions in the workhouse were to be 'less eligible' than those of the worst-off employed man.

The aim was to cut the Gordian knot of rural stagnation by forcing men to look for work rather than face the (highly undesirable) alternative. When applied to the industrial north and west, where periodic unemployment *should* have been relieved by short-term doles, the new system, intended to solve the problem of structural unemployment in the agricultural south, provoked rioting and the burning of the new Bastilles.

The Poor Law Amendment Act attained its first and most limited objective – reduction of the poor rates, which fell in absolute terms, despite the continued increase in population. The relief of rural overpopulation owed more to the new mobility which the railways brought, than to the negative pressures of the workhouse. For nearly a century the 1834 policy dominated official thinking, though humanitarianism, socialism and the disappearance of the Malthusian spectre of overpopulation led to a mitigation of conditions towards the end of the century. The *Report of the Royal Commission on the Poor Law and Unemployment* (1909), however, came out against any fundamental alteration of policy, despite the argument of the Fabian Webbs' *Minority Report* that poverty was the outcome of social arrangements rather than the moral failure of the individual. For another twenty years the shadow of the workhouse and the shame of a pauper's grave were to hang over the casualties of competitive capitalism.

FURTHER READING

Standards of Living

P. Mathias, *The First Industrial Nation, 1700–1914* (London, Methuen, 1969) and E. J. Hobsbawm, *Industry and Empire* (London, Weidenfeld and Nicolson, 1968) have considered the whole period, while P. Deane, *The First Industrial Revolution* (Cambridge University Press, 1965) has covered only the first half.

E. P. Thomson, *The Making of the English Working Class* (London, Gollancz, 1963) is the classic work on the subject, and contains a brilliant chapter on 'Standards and Experiences'.

E. J. Hobsbawm, *Labouring Men* (London, Weidenfeld and Nicolson, 1968) contains a number of essays elaborating his viewpoint.

A. J. Taylor has summarised the debate in an article reprinted in *Essays in Economic History*, ed. E. M. Carus-Wilson, vol. 3.

W. H. B. Court, *British Economic History, 1870–1914* (Cambridge University Press, 1965) is valuable for the later period.

J. Burnett, *A History of the Cost of Living* (Harmondsworth, Penguin, 1969) is packed with figures and fascinating detail.

Labour Organization

H. Pelling, *History of British Trade Unionism* (Harmondsworth, Penguin,

1970) is probably the best and most readily available introduction to the subject.

G. D. H. Cole, *A Short History of the British Working Class Movement, 1789–1947* (London, George Allen and Unwin, 1948) is full of detail and by no means short.

G. D. H. Cole and R. W. Postgate, *The Common People, 1746–1946* (London, Methuen, 1965) is equally lengthy and rather dated in some of its data and interpretations (particularly on wages).

R. Frow and M. Katanka, *A History of British Trade Unionism: A Select Bibliography* (Historical Association, 1969) is a very full bibliography.

M. Bruce, *The Coming of the Welfare State* (London, Batsford, 1961) considers self-help and poverty.

E. Frow and M. Katanka (eds), *1868—Year of the Unions: A Documentary Survey* (1968) is a collection of rare documents.

E. Frow and M. Katanka, *Strikes* (Charles Knight and Co., 1971) is an anthology of first-hand accounts of historic industrial disputes.

There are a number of good collections of essays, notably:

A. Briggs and J. Saville (eds), *Essays in Labour History* (London, Macmillan, 1967).

E. J. Hobsbawm, *Labouring Men* (London, Weidenfeld and Nicolson, 1968).

Chapter 9

EDUCATION

Education has so many aspects that it is impossible in a book of this length even to give an outline of its general development in Britain. Instead we shall have to focus our attention on one particular, and often neglected question – the relationship between education (in the sense of formal, institutionalised instruction) and economic change. Even within the confines of this narrow brief it will be impossible to sketch more than one or two impressions of the more significant features of the nineteenth-century experience.

EDUCATION FOR 'TAKE-OFF'

> The arts (manufactures) which supply the luxuries, conveniences, and necessaries of life, have derived but little advantage from philosophers. In mechanics, for instance, we find that the most important inventions and improvements have been made, not through the reasoning of philosophers, but through the ingenuity of artists (craftsmen) and not unfrequently by common workmen.

This allegation, written in 1798, has become part of the mythology of the Industrial Revolution. In fact the number of truly self-taught geniuses was very small and they were correspondingly well-publicised because contemporaries found them remarkable. Only the careless historian would regard them as typical. The critical invention of the age – Watt's improved engine – was produced by a man who had been fortunate enough to attend one of the finest and most forward-looking universities in Europe.

Elementary education was more widely available in eighteenth-century Britain than has generally been believed. Probably at least two-thirds of the parishes had a village school of some sort, though standards varied considerably, except in Scotland where a system of inspection was already in operation. At the worst, these schools acted as a crèche and, perhaps, imbued their charges with the virtues required of an unlettered labour force – punctuality and a docile ability to perform routine tasks under supervision. Village schools seem to have been more numerous, and more vigorous, in the northern counties, possibly because the example of Scotland was that much nearer, possibly because there were fewer great contrasts of wealth and poverty to depress the ambition of the poor to acquire the rudiments of literacy. Village schooling, followed by a period of apprenticeship to a local craftsman, turned out entrepreneurs like Arkwright, Wedgwood and engineers of the stature of George Stephenson, Joseph Bramah and Richard Trevithick.

What would now be called secondary education was catered for by a variety of institutions – the few great public schools, like Eton and Winchester, which were open only to the sons of the aristocracy, some hundreds of grammar schools, founded or re-founded at the Reformation, which were patronised by the sons of farmers and tradesmen, private boarding schools, run by penurious clergymen. The public schools were sunk in barbarism and brutality and can be ignored. The grammar schools were mostly in decay. It was the Academy that answered the new needs of the day – the private boarding school was but a pale imitation of it.

The most dynamic group in eighteenth-century society, the mercantile and industrial class, found the traditional educational system inadequate for their needs. They resented its concentration on the clergy, the lawyers and the doctors, and, because many were Dissenters, they resented its Church of England bias and exclusiveness. They wanted new forms of knowledge – commercial subjects (book-keeping, modern languages, commercial law) and physical science. Campbell, the author of a careers guide (*The London Tradesman*, 1747) asserted that 'A youth designed for . . . any Mercantile Branch, has no occasion for spending his time at the University, or for a critical knowledge of the Dead Languages . . . .' Most of the successful entrepreneurs would have agreed and so they sent their sons to the new 'Academies', which, at their best, offered an education in every way comparable to that of a university (the academy at Hoxton, for instance, had three Fellows of the Royal Society on its staff). Moreover, they imparted an education which was not only relevant to the demands of commerce but also structured in an appropriate manner, with sandwich courses combining theoretical instruction and practical experience. By the end of the eighteenth century there were some 200 academies in existence – and even those which had originally been intended to cater for the Dissenting ministry, had broadened both their curriculum and their intake in response to the demand for commercial education. The academy at Warrington, one of the most famous, had the eminent Dr Priestley for its guiding spirit, and of 393 students whose careers have been analysed, more than 200 went into commerce and industry, while only 59 became priests. Even the ancient grammar schools began to change under the influence of the academies, and by 1818 it was estimated that 120, with some 10,000 pupils, were offering the new-style of syllabus as an alternative to classical studies.

The English universities, being economically self-sufficient and remote (both geographically and socially) from the centres of Dissenting influence, were less amenable to such pressure. They did teach chemistry and mathematics, but as minor disciplines, and their social exclusiveness limited their students to the offspring of the landed classes. In so far as they did contribute to producing 'scientists', this meant eccentric, aristocratic amateurs, not aggressive, profit-conscious entrepreneurs. The universities of Scotland, however, were centres of true 'enlightenment' and produced such men as Watt, Roebuck, Priestley and Black, who were not only first-rate 'pure' scientists but also keenly interested in the application of scientific knowledge to the problems of industry.

Education, however, is not confined to formal schooling, and the late eighteenth century saw a rich development of aids to learning, chiefly directed at the adult who desired to improve his station in life through knowledge or simply wished to keep up with fashionable new knowledge. Almanacs, textbooks and other works for self-instruction were printed in increasing numbers. Subscription libraries were established in provincial cities like Liverpool and remote rural areas like Pembrokeshire. Itinerant public lecturers, often men of some eminence, such as John Dalton, gave public demonstrations of physical experiments. Their audience consisted mainly of 'polite society', but doubtless a few industrialists attended, perhaps for social rather than economic reasons, though the 'spin-off' effect would still occur whatever the motivation. Count Rumford's 'Royal Institution' gave more permanence to such efforts by providing them with a regular forum.

More significant still were the various provincial learned societies which grew out of informal dining clubs for gentlemen of letters, merchants and manufacturers. The most famous of these was the celebrated Lunar Society, which met every month in Birmingham, and numbered among its members James Watt, Matthew Boulton, Josiah Wedgwood and Erasmus Darwin. Similar societies soon sprang up in Manchester, Newcastle, Derby, Liverpool and Plymouth. Some were literary and philosophical in their orientation, but most met to read and discuss scientific papers, and, in their way, they helped to overcome the major weaknesses of eighteenth-century educational provision – general ignorance of science and wide variations between the state of knowledge in different parts of the country.

The experiences of Josiah Wedgwood provide both a striking example and almost a summary of the pattern of educational provision in the late eighteenth and early nineteenth centuries. Josiah himself had an elementary education which had advanced far enough for him to be described as 'a fair arithmetician and master of a capital hand' at the age of nine, when his father's premature death obliged him to start work in the family firm. At the age of fourteen he entered a formal apprenticeship to learn 'the Art, Mistery, Occupation or Imployment of Throwing and Handleing' and set himself to widen his knowledge by reading and practical experiments. He never lost these habits of self-improvement and discovery and was an enthusiastic member of the Lunar Society. His invention of the pyrometer, a device for measuring very high temperatures, led to his election as a Fellow of the Royal Society.

The education of his sons is also significant. John, the eldest, was sent to an academy in Liverpool, which had been founded by Thomas Bentley, Wedgwood's business associate. He then spent a year at Edinburgh and afterwards went on two tours of the Continent. The second tour, which took him to Rome for a year, was intended to familiarise him with European markets as well as European culture. It served only to strengthen his resolve never to enter the family firm 'as I should thereby lose a great part of the advantage of the liberal education I have received'.

Wedgwood senior had anticipated this and had prepared his younger sons, Tom and Josiah junior, to take over the business in due course. In this he had been advised by a fellow-member of the Lunar Society

I had some talk with Dr Darwin upon my plan of curtailing

> the education of my boys. . . . He approved of the idea, and said he thought it a very idle waste of time for any boys intended for trade to learn Latin, as they seldom learnt it to any tolerable degree of perfection, or retained what they learnt. Besides, they did not want it, and the time would be much better bestowed in making themselves perfect in French and accounts. He advises me not to send them again to Bolton but to teach them what we can at home and then send them to some French academy, unless we can get a French prisoner [from the American war].

Wedgwood did procure a French prisoner, and with the help of Dr Darwin, and the facilities of his work at Etruria, gave the boys the technical and managerial background they needed to take his place.

The example of Wedgwood's sons should remind us that, whatever the contribution of formal education, apprenticeship and 'training on the job' was still regarded as the normal manner in which a young man would be inducted into the methods and mysteries of his occupation. Physicians, lawyers and architects followed well-established patterns of pupilage. New professions, like the civil engineers, gradually evolved their own. Thomas Telford, for instance, was apprenticed to a local builder and represented the generation of self-taught giants. His election as first President of the Institute of Civil Engineers in 1820, however, marks a turning-point. Under his guidance the Institute began to meet to read and discuss practical papers on engineering. It was not long before an accepted corpus of professional knowledge was built up and in its wake came examinations and the whole apparatus of professional status as its exists today. Other new occupational categories, like surveyors and accountants, followed a similar course. The large manufacturing plant served a similar function in training industrial managers. Coalbrookdale, Dowlais and Soho all took in young men who came to learn both the techniques of production and of management. Similar examples can be found in brewing, mining and pottery, though not, significantly, in cotton, a boom industry which was open to all comers, made up its own rules and gave full play to the talents of men like Robert Owen, who at nineteen was manager of a mill with 500 hands. In the early nineteenth century new engineering skills were diffused by former employees, one might almost call them disciples, of men like Bramah and Nasmyth. As Samuel Smiles put it, 'what

Oxford and Cambridge are in letters, workshops such as Maudslay's and Penn's are in mechanics'.

It is difficult to generalise about the relationship between education and economic growth in the critical early phases of industrialisation. The sheer variety of institutions and experiences is bewildering. One or two points, however, stand out. Although the oldest-established schools and universities played almost no part in promoting economic growth and responded but sluggishly to the demands it threw up, new forms of formal provision were established (notably the academies) and a range of ancillary institutions (learned societies, libraries, public lectures, etc.) evolved, between them meeting the thirst for utilitarian knowledge. The continuing importance of apprenticeship and practical training must be emphasised, however, as must the fact that, in most fields, the body of knowledge to be absorbed was incomparably smaller than it is today, because both the economic and technological aspects of manufacturing were still *relatively* unsophisticated.

EDUCATION AND ECONOMIC GROWTH

> Not the external and physical alone is now managed by machinery but the internal and spiritual also. . . . The same habit regulates not our modes of action alone, but our modes of thought and feeling. Men are grown mechanical in heads and heart, as well as in hand (T. Carlyle, *Signs of the Times*, 1829).

The shadow of the factory hung over the schoolroom in the nineteenth century. The relationships between the two are revealing. The spectacular growth of the cotton industry, for instance, exerted a powerful, though indirect, stimulus over the development of mass literacy, by pioneering steam-powered rotary printing and by providing rag waste for paper and cotton cloth for bindings. The result was a flood of cheap books, pamphlets and papers in the two or three decades after Waterloo. But the technology of factory production was perhaps less influential than the organisational principles which underlay its working and inspired the 'monitorial' system of instruction pioneered by Bell and Lancaster. What they did was to apply the principle of division of labour to education, or rather instruction. The teacher taught the monitors who then passed on what they had learned to the mass of younger pupils. Coleridge hailed this new mode of teaching as 'a vast moral steam-engine'. The metaphor is significant – the system reduced knowledge to a product and children to the level of automatons. Robert Lowe's 'payment by results' campaign in the 1860s was based on similar assumptions – his defence was that it would achieve efficiency in a demonstrable manner and, failing that, it would at least be cheap. It was an argument calculated to appeal to a calculating age.

Educational provision for the mass of workers was extended, piece-meal and with some hesitation, throughout the nineteenth century. Robert Owen led the way at New Lanark, pioneering visual aids, learning by doing and creative play. His methods were not widely adopted, although a number of other manufacturers (particularly in Scotland) did set up schools for the children of their employees. Attempts to extend such provision as part of general factory legislation were largely unsuccessful: most manufacturers saw no point, or rather profit, in it. In the main, elementary education for the masses was left in the hands of two voluntary bodies, the National and the British and Foreign Schools Society, the one sponsored by the Church of England, and the other by the Nonconformist churches. The government started subsidising their efforts in 1833, and within a quarter of a century was paying out almost £500,000 a year. More direct action was precluded by the storms that were bound to arise between the two factions whenever anything threatened the *modus vivendi* they had established. Even the famous Elementary Education Act of 1870 only attempted to plug the gaps in the voluntary system by establishing Board Schools where necessary. Religious disputes continued to hamper development in this area well into the twentieth century.

And yet there was a desperate need for elementary education. Urban growth had created vast agglomerations of people, without even the meagre services of the old village schools. Methodism, Sunday Schools and Schools of Industry had, for a variety of motives, spread basic literacy more widely. Indeed, the many local censuses of the period 1815–35 suggest that about two-thirds of factory workers could read, though perhaps not very well, and probably less than half of these could write as well. The question of whether they should be educated at all was keenly debated, but, significantly, with little or no reference to economic considerations (e.g. that the growing use of machinery in industry made literacy among workmen desirable). The relevant criteria were social and moral. Opponents of popular education argued that literacy would enable the poor to read subversive literature, like

Cobbet's *Twopenny Trash* or *Black Dwarf*: supporters of mass education countered with the assertion that literacy would enable the poor to read the Bible and that a thorough instruction in Christian principles would teach them to acknowledge their lowly station in the order of things. The latter argument eventually prevailed, but it meant that the main object of elementary education in the nineteenth century was not to discover and develop the latent talent of the poor, but to keep it safely slumbering.

More significant, perhaps, from the point of view of economic growth, was the establishment of Mechanics Institutes, where artisans could learn more about their craft and the theoretical principles behind it, through attendance at evening lectures and the use of reading-room facilities. The London Mechanics Institute was founded in 1824 by George Birkbeck who had delivered a successful series of scientific lectures to an audience of working men in Edinburgh. Within twenty years there were some 200 Mechanics Institutes with 50,000 members, but they had lost their original character and purpose. Swamped by white-collar workers (like clerks and shopkeepers) and eager for self-improvement, they lost their artisan audience, many of whom had anyway regarded the whole venture as an employers' plot to distract them from radical politics. By the 1850s these institutes had lost their impetus and had begun to wither away.

It was about this time that the first serious criticisms of English education at the higher levels and on economic grounds began to emerge. The Great Exhibition of 1851 had demonstrated British industrial supremacy to the world, but the Paris Universal Exhibition of 1855 gave rise to unfavourable comparisons between the theoretical knowledge of French and German workmen and their English counterparts. In the same year, Michael Faraday, lecturing to an audience which included the Prince Consort, delivered a scathing attack on traditional, classical education which failed to teach even the simplest principles of chemistry or mechanics. (Gladstone is a case in point – a brilliant scholar who distinguished himself in Homeric and Biblical studies and the complex field of taxation, but who stubbornly refused to have anything to do with science.) Faraday closed by reminding his audience that the technological developments which were shaping the character of the age – the railway, the electric telegraph and the steam-engine – had been developed by men whom circumstances had denied the 'benefits' of a grounding in the classics.

In 1864 a Royal Commission gave these general criticisms greater point:

> Nor would it be wise in a country whose continued prosperity so greatly depends upon its ability to maintain its pre-eminence in manufactures to neglect the application of natural science to the industrial arts . . .

There was only one way to do this, through education, and no one agitated more for reform in this direction than William Lyon Playfair. In 1867 he had served as a judge at the Paris Exhibition and on his return he wrote to Lord Taunton, then Chairman of the Schools Inquiry Commission:

> I am sorry to say that, with very few exceptions, a singular accordance of opinion prevailed that our country had shown little inventiveness and made but little progress in the peaceful arts of industry . . . the one cause upon which there was most unanimity of conviction is that France, Prussia, Austria, Belgium and Switzerland possess good systems of industrial education for the masters and managers of factories and workshops and that England possesses none.

The reasons are not difficult to discover. The universities sponsored little research. Even the self-consciously utilitarian University of London, founded in 1826 to promote science and other modern studies, was largely concerned with medicine. State assistance was hampered by the unwillingness of the (still influential) landed interest to subsidise a form of knowledge they either regarded with contempt or saw as a threat to their own position. *The Economist* strongly condemned 'the ambition and greediness of those who beg in the name of science', and it was not until 1890 that the first State grant to scientific research was made and even in 1901 the Exchequer contribution was limited to £25,000 a year.

Manufacturers were equally unwilling to help themselves. Largely untutored in the formal sense, they liked to believe that the old 'rule of thumb' methods which had served their fathers and grandfathers could still hold good. Most would have endorsed Samuel Smiles's view that 'the career of industry which the nation has pursued, has also provided its best education. . . . In the school of labour is taught the best practical wisdom.' They saw no reason to pay for research which might benefit their rivals, and were unwilling for their employees to congregate for instruction lest they should give away 'trade secrets'. When the pressure of foreign competition led to a Parliamentary inquiry into technical education (which resulted in the Technical Education Act of 1889) a north-east coast shipbuilder told an audience of fellow engineers:

> Much has been said in recent years about technical education. ... In our own arts I can conceive of no better school than the workshop. You have there the experience and skill of the best artisans, you have the feeling of being engaged in serious constructions, you are in the very atmosphere of your craft.

The old, almost mystical, faith in empiricism and practical experience continued almost undisturbed.

Nor did any response come from the great schools. At Rugby, the earnest Dr Arnold had, between 1828 and 1842, effected a revolution. His principles were widely imitated in the new and rejuvenated public schools which dominated upper-class education, and values, throughout the century. His primary emphasis was upon Christian ethics and the development of character through sport and personal responsibility (e.g. as a prefect). Intellectual attainments were valued, but they were secondary. Modern studies might be admitted to the curriculum, but the classics remained essential for the making of a Gentleman. His son, the poet, critic (and Inspector of Schools) Matthew Arnold, told the University of Cambridge that 'for the majority of mankind a little of mathematics goes a long way', and in one of his more light-hearted works he poked fun at the curriculum of the Academy of a mythical 'Dr Silverpump':

> None of your antiquated rubbish – all practical work – latest discoveries in science – mind constantly kept excited – lots of interesting experiments – lights of all colours – fizz, fizz, bang, bang. That's what I call forming a man.

The public-school ethic, as it developed, exalted the liberal professions and the ideal of service to State and Empire. This turned young men (including the heirs of industrialists, ambitious for their sons' *social* advancement) away from trade and industry, which were 'vulgar'. American values were in direct contrast. There, the self-made businessman was a popular folk-hero and well respected in society, as he had been to some extent in early Victorian England, when the nation was still intoxicated by the achievements of industry. The result was that Britain had the wisest judges and most devoted civil servants, but the United

States had the most dynamic men of business (and some of the most corrupt judges and civil servants). It might reasonably be objected that the number of people who attended public schools was very small, but they did hold the key positions in an industrial sector still largely controlled by family firms.

Employers' attitudes were crucial. Either because they still upheld the traditional faith in the old ways or because a public-school education had caused them to regard the family firm as an estate to be milked rather than an enterprise to be developed, they remained largely hostile to the development of technical education. The Board of Education annual report for 1908–9 concluded that:

> The slow growth of [institutions for higher technology] is ... in the main to be ascribed to the small demand in this country for the services of young men well trained in the theoretical side of industrial operations and in the sciences underlying them. There still exists among the generation of employers, a strong preference for the man trained from an early age in the works, and a prejudice against the so-called 'college-trained' man.

The main issue of education in relation to science and industry, which was vital to Britain's industrial future, was never squarely faced or properly settled, despite a vast amount of public discussion. Nor did the problem ever engage the attention of a statesman of first rank throughout the whole century. After 1870 or so, British industrial growth came up against a number of limitations, some of which were, perhaps, insuperable. Appropriate educational provision does not fall into this category, however, and failure in this field was all the more damaging because its effects were so pervasive. The economic failures of the twentieth century have their roots in the educational negligence of the past.

FURTHER READING

W. H. G. Armytage, *400 Years of English Education* (Cambridge University Press, 1964) is a clearly sub-divided textbook.

S. Pollard, *The Genesis of Modern Management* (London, Edward Arnold, 1965) deals with the educational opportunities available to eighteenth-century entrepreneurs.

W. H. B. Court, *British Economic History, 1870–1914* (Cambridge University Press, 1965) contains extracts from a number of the reports and recommendations on technical education.

Chapter 10

FINANCE

Economic activity needs two sorts of capital – fixed capital (like machinery), which pays for itself over a long period, and circulating capital, for the payment of wages and the purchase of raw materials. The requirements of entrepreneurs vary with the nature of their business – an industrialist, for instance, will require a larger amount of fixed capital than a merchant. An entrepreneur wishing to expand his activities beyond what his personal resources can support, must borrow capital. If he seeks a loan to launch a major enterprise involving new plant and buildings, he will need to borrow from a long-term lender. If, on the other hand, he only needs cash to tide him over a temporary crisis until, say, he makes a large sale, he will need to borrow from a short-term lender. The former operates on a time-scale of years, the latter of months or even weeks. The institutional framework which supports the activities of long-term lenders are known as the capital market, of short-term lenders as the money market. Nowadays their activities overlap and mesh together, but they developed quite independently of one another.

THE MONEY MARKET

The main lenders of short-term funds are banks. The first bankers were London goldsmiths who, in the seventeenth century, held depositors cash in safe-keeping, for a fee. Finding that customers never wished to withdraw all their cash at once, they began to loan out a proportion at interest and then to pay interest (at a lower rate than they charged) to attract more funds from depositors to enable them to extend their lending activities. By 1800 about seventy London banks had grown up in this way, and many were already specialists in a particular branch of business, such as arranging credit for overseas trade, buying and selling bullion or raising loans for the government.

Public Revenue, 1700–1909

Year	Customs and Excise		Land and assessed taxes		Property and income tax		Death duties		Rest		Total	
	£m.	%	£m.	%	£m.	%	£m.	%	£m.	%	£m.	%
					—	—	—	—				
					—	—	—	—				
					—	—	—	—				
					—	—	—	—				
					—	—	—	—				
					—	—	—	—				
					—	—	—	—				
					—	—	—	—				
					—	—	—	—				
1790–9	13.7	65	3.6	17	0.2	1	—	—	3.5	17	21.0	
1800–9	29.6	59	4.9	10	5.6	11	—	—	10.2	20	50.3	
1810–19	40.8	58	8.0	11	11.1	16	—	—	10.3	15	70.2	
1820–9	41.2	71	6.5	11	—	—	—	—	10.5	18	58.2	
1830–9	38.2	74	4.7	9	—	—	—	—	8.7	17	51.6	
1840–9	37.3	68	4.4	8	3.3	6	—	—	10.1	18	55.1	
1850–9	39.3	63	3.6	6	8.8	14	—	—	10.5	17	62.2	
1860–9	42.4	62	3.3	5	8.6	12	—	—	14.4	21	68.7	
1870–9	46.1	61	2.7	4	6.7	9	5.4	7	14.1	19	75.0	
1880–9	45.8	53	2.9	3	12.3	14	7.3	9	17.8	21	86.1	
1890–9	51.5	49	2.5	2	15.2	15	12.0	12	23.1	22	104.3	
1900–9	68.0	45	2.6	2	31.1	21	18.0	12	30.9	20	150.6	

Note: Great Britain 1700–1800 / United Kingdom 1801–1909 } figures for central government only.

Source: B. R. Mitchell and P. Deane (1962), Cambridge University Press, pp. 386–8, 392–5.

Public Expenditure, 1700–1909

Year	National Debt (cumulative)	Total debt charges		Military expenditure		Civil government		(Education)		Total	
	£m.	£m.	%	£m.	%	£m.	%	£m.	%	£m.	%
								—	—		
								—	—		
								—	—		
								—	—		
								—	—		
								—	—		
								—	—		
								—	—		
								—	—		
1790–9	426.6	11.6	35	19.4	58	1.9	6	—	—	33.4	
1800–9	599.0	20.0	33	35.3	59	4.6	6	(0.1)	0	60.6	
1810–19	844.3	28.5	35	47.0	58	5.5	7	(0.2)	0	81.3	
1820–9	801.3	30.4	59	15.7	30	5.6	11	(0.1)	0	51.8	
1830–9	788.2	28.9	58	13.1	26	4.9	10	(0.1)	0	49.7	
1840–9	794.3	29.2	57	15.1	30	6.1	12	(0.3)	1	51.0	
1850–9	808.8	28.4	47	21.9	37	7.9	13	(0.7)	1	59.6	
1860–9	751.0	26.6	41	26.7	41	10.7	16	(1.3)	2	64.6	
1870–9	736.1	26.2	40	24.3	37	13.5	20	(2.6)	4	66.1	
1880–9	623.8	27.6	36	28.0	37	18.7	24	(4.9)	6	76.7	
1890–9	598.7	23.6	26	36.4	40	20.2	22	(9.2)	10	89.2	
1900–9	716.1	23.2	16	79.1	55	30.2	21	(14.9)	10	143.6	

In the eighteenth century banks began to develop in the provinces. Only a dozen or so existed before 1750, but by the end of the century the quickening pace of economic life had given birth to some 400. Most of these had developed from the activities of small businessmen (butchers, brewers, iron-masters) who managed to accumulate surplus funds, learned how to loan them to advantage and were able to build up the financial side of their business by accepting deposits from local landowners or businessmen. Both Barclays and Lloyds originated in this way. These 'country banks' helped business by lending 'on call' to manufacturers and merchants who were temporarily short of cash and by arranging for payments to be made over long distances by credit transfer arrangements (e.g. bills of exchange) which cheated the highwayman of a dishonest living. By arrangement with London banks, the country banks in rural areas could channel surplus funds from agriculture (e.g. after the harvest) towards profitable opportunities to loan to merchants and manufacturers in ports or industrial areas who needed short-term credit.

The banking system at the beginning of the nineteenth century, despite its proven value to commerce and industry, had a number of weaknesses:

1. The law forbade banks (except the Bank of England, the government's bank) to organise as joint-stock companies; they were compelled to operate as individuals or partnerships (with not more than six partners), which limited the funds they could accumulate and hence both the extent of their activities and their stability when a crisis of confidence induced a large number of depositors to simultaneously withdraw their money.

2. Because partners' liability was unlimited (i.e. if the business foundered, its creditors could claim not only all its assets but also the private fortunes and estates of all the partners), they were wary of establishing branches beyond their personal supervision. This confined their activities to one locality and often made them more vulnerable by tying their interests to one or two local industries

---

Note:

(i) Figures for Great Britain 1700–1800, United Kingdom, 1801–1909.

(ii) Figures for central government only. All figures, except col. 1, annual average per decade.

Source: B. R. Mitchell and P. Deane (1962), Cambridge University Press, pp. 389–91, 396–9, 401–3.

which could strain their slender resources to breaking-point during a depression.

3. Banking technique was still undeveloped and bankers could only use trial and error to gauge the proportion of deposits which might safely be loaned out. Error could result in bankruptcy. This could also happen if a large proportion of the bank's assets was in mortgages, property or other securities which could not be swiftly realised for cash in a 'liquidity crisis'.

4. The volume of coinage in circulation was inadequate to keep pace with the expansion of the economy. Entrepreneurs were driven to a variety of expedients like issuing their own money ('trade tokens'), which was illegal, paying their employees in kind ('truck'), which could be abused, or paying them in large coins every month instead of small ones every week, which made budgeting for the workers very difficult. (One manufacturer thought of the ingenious solution of staggering payment. A group of his workers was paid in the morning and went to the shops, where the small change was shortly afterwards exchanged for notes by the manufacturer's pay clerk who then used the coins to pay the next group of workers and so on.) In these circumstances the country banks performed a real service by issuing banknotes (paper promises to pay coin on demand), which circulated freely as money. Bankruptcy would, of course, render such notes worthless. During the period 1797–1821 the government's decision to suspend convertibility of notes enabled banks to issue notes at their discretion. The volume of paper currency thus expanded far faster than the amount of goods and services, creating rapid inflation.

5. The Bank of England enjoyed a monopoly of joint-stock banking and offered its services to only a limited range of (London) customers (e.g. chartered trading companies like the East India Company).

In Scotland, where the legal system permitted joint-stock banks, the system was far more stable. Credit facilities were more easily available, even to small businessmen, and the notes issued by sound managements enjoyed general confidence as bank failures were virtually unknown. Improvement in the English system perforce waited on two related developments:

1. A change in the Bank of England's status from that of a large and privileged bank to that of a central bank, assuming responsi-

bility for the management of the currency and acting as lender of last resort, i.e. becoming the banker's bank.

2. Extension of the Bank of England's joint-stock privileges to include other banks.

The transformation came gradually – partly through the initiative of the Bank, partly under the pressure of government and the clamour of the business community, and largely as a result of a series of financial crises.

In 1825 a general liquidity crisis made forty-five banks bankrupt before the Bank of England relieved the situation by releasing reserves of currency to satisfy depositors' demands for cash (mostly obsolete gold guineas and banknotes of less than £5 denomination withdrawn in 1821). The Bank had acted as lender of last resort, but tardily, and legislation in 1826 obliged it to open branches in major provincial towns and authorised the establishment of joint-stock banks outside a sixty-five-mile radius of London. In 1833 such banks were allowed within the radius, providing they issued no notes. Aggressive in their attitude and progressive in their methods, the joint-stock banks grew by multiplying their branches and offering their facilities to ever-wider sections of the middle class.

In 1844 the Bank Charter Act attempted to prevent inflationary crises by limiting note issue. Private banks were allowed to issue no more than was in circulation at that date and were to lose the right to issue notes if they amalgamated or opened a London office. The Bank of England was allowed to issue as many notes as it could back to their full value with bullion, plus a 'fiduciary issue' (backed by securities not gold) initially fixed at £14,000,000. The effect of the Act was to place the Bank of England in a key position to manage the currency. It put an end to banknote inflation but provided no safeguard against the over-extension of credit, and took no account of the need to provide an abnormally large volume of currency at periodic intervals of crisis. This was revealed in 1847 when the cessation of the railway boom and the high prices of imported grain and cotton caused by bad harvests, produced a run on the banks for cash. It was sufficient, however, for the government to allow the Bank to ignore the limits of the fiduciary issue for the panic to subside. When a similar crisis arose in 1857 (because the discount houses had irresponsibly accepted a large number of dubious bills of exchange), it did prove necessary to exceed the limit before the crisis could be brought under control.

THE CAPITAL MARKET

Long-term credit in the eighteenth century was extended to either the state – the safest, since 1689, of all debtors – or joint-stock companies, which had obtained their privilege by a Royal Charter or an Act of Parliament on the grounds that they were either merchant ventures entailing high risks which must be widely spread to be accepted (e.g. Hudson's Bay Company) or some form of enterprise which would benefit the public but be beyond the resources of any partnership to set up (e.g. a turnpike trust, canal, bridge, water, gas or insurance company). Joint-stock companies enjoyed the following advantages:

1. Division of their capital into saleable, transferable shares.
2. 'Legal personality', allowing the company to sue (e.g. debtors) as a company and not through any one shareholder or officer.
3. Limited liability.

Dealings in shares were conducted by stockbrokers (buying and selling on behalf of clients) and stock-jobbers (dealing on their own account) who operated at first in London coffee houses and, after 1801, in their own Stock Exchange. In the nineteenth century the range of securities they dealt in widened, particularly as a result of the speculative boom of 1824–5, the railway 'manias' and the growing trend towards investment abroad.

However, the ordinary industrialist remained shut out of this market, which was London-based and increasingly oriented to the demands of overseas trade and investment. The industrialist perforce did what he had always done – saved, borrowed from friends, relatives, fellow church-goers, established industrialists and possibly the occasional merchant or landowner. Growth was financed through 'plough-back' of profits, a practice which caused him to regard demands for higher wages with a jaundiced eye. This self-financing technique served well enough in the early phases of industrialisation when the role of fixed capital was relatively limited and banks and dealers would extend credit to cover wages and raw material costs, the major burdens of outlay. But as the drive to mechanisation and larger plant got under way, the need to mobilise more long-term capital became imperative and the attractions of the joint-stock form of organisation greater. Public opinion extracted the necessary legislation from governments which still retained the lawyer's (at the time not unjustified) suspicion that a joint-stock company was a charlatan's device for swindling the innocent of 'blind' capital.

In 1837 incorporation of joint-stock companies by letters patent became possible. This administrative procedure was cheaper than a private Act of Parliament, but the company had to supply particulars to a registrar who made them available for public inspection. In 1844 joint-stock status became available to all companies making statutory disclosures to the registrar, but neither of these measures was satisfactory because they did not confer limited liability status. So long as it remained generally unavailable, investors would hesitate to employ surplus capital productively in industry or contribute to social amelioration through building societies or trustee savings banks. A Royal Commission opposed general availability but its objections were overborne and between 1856 and 1861 it was extended to enterprises of every kind. An Act of 1862 codified these piece-meal measures.

PERFECTION OF THE CREDIT MECHANISM

1825, 1847 and 1857 had been years of crisis. Each had swept away unsound ventures (135 firms had collapsed in three months in 1857) but, having shaken established financial institutions, had left them stronger and more efficient. The crisis of 1866 was to prove even more traumatic than its predecessors, but the long-term effects were beneficial.

The root cause of the crisis of 1866 was a relatively new phenomenon, the investment finance company, an institution devoted to the provision of initial capital for new entrepreneurs with novel processes and techniques to exploit. Investment finance companies, however, had to raise capital for their operations and they did so by borrowing funds at interest and 'on call'. In other words, they borrowed short and lent long, inevitably risking a major liquidity crisis.

The most prominent investment finance company was that promoted by the discount house of Overend, Gurney & Co. The death of the millionaire Quaker Gurney in 1857 allowed the firm to pass into the hands of an irresponsible directorate which recklessly pumped money into new enterprises in the heady days of the early 1860s. In 1864–5 the investment finance companies began to lose the confidence of depositors, who were worried by rumours of heavy over-commitment. Early in 1866 a firm with a name similar to Overend's went bankrupt. A panic started and in May, Overend, Gurney & Co. was ruined because the Bank of England, which held the discount houses responsible for the crash of 1857 and disapproved of their venturing into the field of long-term credit, refused to help them. This attitude rid the market of these unsound institutions but brought ruin to many investors.

The last great crisis of the century saw the Bank of England intervene to rescue the money market rather than abandon it to its fate. While it is generally true that defaults on foreign investments were rare, this was truer of some areas than others. In South America violent changes of government were likely to lead to the repudiation of debts incurred by the previous régime. When such a crisis threatened to occur in Argentina in 1890 the implications for British finance were potentially disastrous. Investment in railways, docks and meat-packing plant had quadrupled British holdings in the Argentine in a mere five years. Much of this flow of capital had been handled by Baring Brothers, one of the City's greatest merchant bankers. They secretly disclosed to the Bank of England that should a default occur they had so far overlent on their realisable assets that they would be temporarily illiquid. The Bank, having assured itself that Barings still held enough long-term assets to be considered solvent, arranged for a consortium of London bankers and discount houses to collectively guarantee Barings' liabilities. By the time rumours of crisis began to circulate, the rescue operation was complete and the nation was saved from being 'within twenty-four hours of barter'. The Bank of England had not only assumed the full role of central bank by asserting its leadership of the money market, it had also acted with skill and discretion to prevent a major panic from ever starting.

Joint-stock organisation spread throughout industry, particularly from the 1880s, as the scale of plant required increased. Old-established branches of manufacture, like cotton-spinning, where family firms were the rule, were slow to 'go public', though many became private limited companies after an Act of 1907 gave explicit recognition to this new form of organisation. Industries which did adopt joint-stock organisation quickly found that it implied a new division between ownership, vested in thousands of relatively small and anonymous shareholders, and management, vested in a new class of professional controllers of resources. The emergence of the modern international corporation had begun.

FURTHER READING

It is unlikely that many students will wish to delve far into this field. Most examination questions on this topic are fairly straightforward and can be dealt with from a knowledge of the relevant chapters in P. Deane (11), P. Mathias (13) and S. G. Checkland (6). All three contain bibliographies of books and articles on this subject.

Chapter 11

THE ROLE OF GOVERNMENT

Quesnay was a French 'philosophe', a physician to Louis XV. When the king said to him 'What would you do if you were king?', he replied, 'Nothing'. 'Then who would rule?' 'The Laws'. This was a classic statement of the basic premiss of *laissez-faire* – that human affairs were governed by 'natural laws'. The task of government was to discover those laws and to allow them free play. Newton in the seventeenth century had uncovered the laws behind the behaviour of matter. The task of succeeding generations should be to uncover the laws which underlay the behaviour of man.

These ideas were formulated at length in Adam Smith's great work, *The Wealth of Nations* (1776) which set out the following arguments:

1. All men seek their own best interest and are the best judge of that interest.
2. If men gave free rein to their self-interest (assumed to be the same as their material advantage) society *as a whole* would benefit, even though the selfish individuals of which it was composed had no such intention.
3. All government interference, however well-intentioned, could only obstruct the free play of these 'natural laws'.
4. Britain should, therefore, abandon her ancient traditions of government intervention and abolish:

   (i) tariffs on imported goods;
   (ii) regulation of wages and prices;
   (iii) monopoly trading rights (e.g. the East India Company).

Many of the laws which Smith protested against were inoperative anyway, but his arguments were extremely attractive to the dynamic mercantile manufacturing classes. The French wars (1793–1815) delayed their introduction by putting a premium on government activity, but *laissez-faire* ideas soon exerted a strong influence on government policy.

1813 – The East India Company loses monopoly of India trade (of China trade 1833).

1814 – Statute of Artificers repealed.

1825 – Bubble Act repealed. Laws against export of machinery and emigration of skilled artisans repealed.

1842–5 – Peel's Free Trade Budgets abolish tariffs on raw materials and reduce those on manufactures and semi-manufactures to minimal levels.

1846 – Corn Laws repealed.

1849 – Navigation Laws abolished.

1854 – Coastal Shipping thrown open to all.

1860 – Free Trade treaty (Cobden–Chevalier treaty) between England and France.

On the other hand the problems of an industrialising, urbanising society created pressures which demanded *increasing* government intervention:

1. Factory Acts (1833, 1847) regulated hours and conditions of labour in mills, as the Mines and Collieries Act (1842) regulated conditions underground.
2. Public Health Acts (1848, 1875) empowered Local Authorities to provide water supply and drainage and control building.
3. Similar measures controlled emigrant ships (Passenger Acts) conditions on merchant ships (the inauguration of the 'Plimsoll' Line, 1876) food adulteration, railway safety, etc.

This legislation was, however, largely regulatory and negative, involving little expenditure and no transfer of incomes from rich to poor. It was concerned almost entirely with the correction of abuses, not the positive promotion of socially desirable conditions. Throughout the century the Victorian state remained hampered by:

1. The lack of a large, efficient, uncorrupt bureacracy (at least until after the introduction of entry by competitive examination in 1870).
2. The lack of adequate funds (given the contemporary statesman's obsession with 'economy' in government spending).
3. The general belief in the positive virtue of 'Self-Help'.

4. The general opposition to state action which was popularly associated with 'French slavery'.

Therefore in the most fundamental respects, the nineteenth century was an age of *laissez-faire*:

1. Towns and railways were unplanned and built with much waste.
2. Education and health remained largely in the hands of the churches and charities.
3. The free flow of capital was unrestricted. No attempt was made, for instance, to turn foreign investment into a weapon for diplomacy.
4. Protection was abandoned completely after 1846 (until 1931).
5. Emigration was not even directed towards the Empire.

Even the socialistic measures of the Liberal government of 1905–14 (old-age pensions, National Insurance, labour exchanges) involved no significant transfers of incomes. The National Insurance Scheme (1911) for instance, was intended to finance itself like any commercial insurance scheme.

Not until the Great War showed that government control could work and the post-war depression showed that it was necessary, did *laissez-faire* assumptions cease to be the basis of official policy.

FURTHER READING

A. J. Taylor, *Laissez-Faire and State Intervention in Nineteenth-Century Britain* (London, Macmillan, Studies in Economic History series) is the obvious starting point.

Asa Briggs, *The Age of Improvement* (London, Longmans, 1959) and G. Kitson Clark, *The Making of Victorian England* (London, Methuen, 1966) are both good general texts. They cover much of the ground and highlight the philosophies behind the policies.

S. G. Checkland, *The Rise of Industrial Society in England, 1815–85* (London, Longmans, 1964) contains an excellent discussion of government (Chapter 9: 'The Politics of an Industrialising Society').

P. Deane, *The First Industrial Revolution* (Cambridge University Press, 1965), Chapter 13, and P. Mathias, *The First Industrial Nation, 1700–1914* (London, Methuen, 1969), Chapter 3, both contain expositions of the relationship between state activity and economic growth.

The last three books contain full bibliographies.

Chapter 12

THE STRUCTURE OF SOCIETY

The social structure of the pre-industrial world was a complex hierarchy, based on rank and order. Gregory King's analysis, drawn up at the end of the seventeenth century, starts with 'Dukes' and works down through the ranks of the aristocracy to 'great merchants', members of the 'liberal professions', those who styled themselves 'Gent.' or 'Esquire' (meaningful titles then, not democratic courtesies) and finally to common 'husbandmen', 'cottagers' and paupers. Nowadays most of us think in terms of a social structure based on three broad 'classes', an image of society which was the product of industrialisation and which, according to Asa Briggs, emerged in the period between 1780 and 1830. Victorian railways reflected this tripartite division by offering first-, second- and third-class accommodation. Matthew Arnold regarded the society of which he was so critical as being divided into the Barbarians, the Philistines and the Populace. This threefold division is easy to comprehend and has been almost unconsciously absorbed into conventional modes of thought. For this reason it will be used as the framework for this chapter, but the limitations of this concept and the important distinctions it conceals should also become apparent.

For instance, differences between one part of the country and another remained significant. Consider the observations of that acute Frenchman, Alexis de Tocqueville, on contrasting social conditions in two great industrial cities:

> At Manchester a few great capitalists, thousands of poor workmen and little middle class. At Birmingham, few large industries, many small industrialists. At Manchester workmen are counted by the thousand, 2,000 or 3,000 in the factories. At Birmingham the workers work in their own houses or in little workshops in company with the master himself. . . . From the look of the inhabitants of Manchester, the working people

of Birmingham seem more healthy, better off, more orderly and more moral than those of Manchester.

To call the nineteenth century 'an age of transition' is to label it with a historical cliché. The study of change is the historian's business and therefore any age that he studies has features which might lead him to regard it as 'transitional'. Nevertheless, the label is peculiarly appropriate for the nineteenth century, which saw a definite change both in the structure of society and in the image that various social groups had of it and of their place in it. It was self-consciously an age of progress, and progress was interpreted in terms of social as well as technological advance. A high level of social mobility had long been regarded, by foreigners and Englishmen alike, as one of the peculiar features of English society. In 1767 it was noted that:

> In England the several ranks of men slide into each other almost imperceptibly. . . . Hence arises a strong emulation in all the several stations and conditions to vie with each other; and a perpetual restless ambition in each of the inferior ranks to raise themselves to the level of those immediately above them.

As we have seen, mid-Victorian Britain erected an ideology of 'Self-Help' on the basis of this social phenomenon. Individual self-assertion through an accepted code of economic behaviour was regarded with admiration and approval as the key to national economic growth and an infallible indication of personal moral worth. A Nottingham businessman, addressing the British Association meeting at Liverpool, enunciated this creed as follows:

> If any one intends to improve his condition, he must earn all he can, spend as little as he can and make what he does spend bring him and his family all the real enjoyments he can. The first saving which a working man effects out of his earnings, is the first step, and because it is the first step, the most important step towards true independence. Now independence is as practicable in the case of an industrious and economic, though originally poor, workman, as in that of the tradesman or merchant. . . .

Increased social mobility, the redefinition of the relationships between different social groups, and the growth of class consciousness (most acute in the period 1830–48 and also, perhaps, in the 1880s and 1900s) led to nation-wide movements of social protest, manifested in various campaigns for social and economic justice. And yet there was no social revolution, though Marx had confidently anticipated it as the inevitable fate of the pioneer of industrial capitalism. The absence of social cataclysm can be attributed – at least, in part – to the fact that emigration siphoned off potentially dangerous elements, while the talented and ambitious who chose to remain in Britain were denatured as potential revolutionaries by the cults of 'respectability' and 'self-improvement'. Thus generalised discontent was deprived of the cadres of local leaders it needed to convert energy into action. It was neither guns nor prison camps which saved Victorian Britain from revolution, but Sunday schools and 'temperance beverages'.

THE EMERGENCE OF THE WORKING CLASS

In the eighteenth century the term 'working class' was unknown. The members of this class were usually referred to as 'the labouring poor' or, more simply, 'the poor'. They made up the bulk of the population, and most property-owners were conscious of their vulnerability as prosperous islands in an ocean of economic wretchedness, hence the influence of Malthus's scarifying predictions of the dangers of 'pampering' the poor. The social impact of industrialisation heightened their apprehensions by agglomerating the poor into vast, chaotic masses and subjecting them to traumatic new pressures.

It was the poor who suffered the main impact of economic transformation. Immigration to towns meant the loss of friends and relatives and the abandonment of a traditional rural culture. Even more devastating were the disruptions involved in the switch from agricultural or domestic modes of production to the novel methods of the factory. The rhythm of the seasons was replaced by the rhythm of the machine. The clock and the bell imposed a new order and automation-like regularity upon daily life. Old skills and knowledge became redundant and traditional income differentials disappeared. Monotonous work, the social function of which was by no means immediately apparent, degraded employees to the level of 'hands'. Pride and self-respect suffered. Grave tensions emerged within the family as earnings capacity was no longer related to age or experience. Depersonalisation of social and working relationships, and the loss of the old restraints imposed by squire and parson, encouraged unstable patterns of social

Occupation Structure, 1851. Principal occupation groups in Britain in 1851 in order of size

	Male	*Female*
Total population	10,224,000	10,736,000
Population of ten years old and upwards	7,616,000	8,155,000
Agriculture: farmer, grazier, labourer, servant	1,563,000	227,000
Domestic service (excluding farm service)	134,000	905,000
Cotton worker, every kind, with printer, dyer	255,000	272,000
Building craftsman: carpenter, bricklayer, mason, plasterer, plumber, etc.	442,000	1,000
Labourer (unspecified)	367,000	9,000
Milliner, dressmaker, seamstress (seamster)	494	340,000
Wool worker, every kind, with carpet-weaver	171,000	113,000
Shoe-maker	243,000	31,000
Coal-miner	216,000	3,000
Tailor	135,000	18,000
Washerwoman		145,000
Seaman (merchant), pilot	144,000	
Silk worker	53,000	80,000
Blacksmith	112,000	592
Linen, flax worker	47,000	56,000
Carter, carman, coachman, postboy, cabman, busman, etc.	83,000	1,000
Iron worker, founder, moulder (excluding iron-mining, nails, hardware, cutlery, files, tools, machines)	79,000	590
Railway driver, etc., porter, etc., labourer, platelayer	65,000	54
Hosiery worker	35,000	30,000
Lace worker	10,000	54,000
Machine, boiler maker	63,000	647
Baker	56,000	7,000
Copper, tin, lead-miner	53,000	7,000
Charwoman		55,000
Commercial clerk	44,000	19
Fisherman	37,000	1,000
Miller	37,000	562
Earthenware worker	25,000	11,000
Sawyer	35,000	23
Shipwright, boat-builder, block and mast maker	32,000	28
Straw-plait worker	4,000	28,000
Wheelwright	30,000	106
Glover	4,500	25,000
Nailer	19,000	10,000
Iron-miner	27,000	910
Tanner, currier, fellmonger	25,000	276
Printer	22,000	222

behaviour – petty crime, drunkenness and vice – which were such a deplorable aspect of the 'condition of England' question in the 1840s. Equally deplorable in the eyes of middle-class reformers were the careless budgeting and irrational extravagance of the 'lower orders', which not only ran directly counter to the current utilitarian emphasis on calculation and the respected virtue of thrift, but seemed all the more lunatic now that the working man had become completely dependent on money wages for his income.

This dislocation of established social patterns was by no means a uniform process over the whole country. Self-sufficient groups like the miners and seamen preserved their peculiar identity well into the twentieth century, and, indeed, close examination of the mid-Victorian social structure reveals the complex hierarchy prevailing *within* the 'working classes', a hierarchy which was itself subject to important regional variations; London, for instance, was almost the only town with a large class of 'costermongers' (street traders). At the summit of this social pyramid stood the 'aristocracy of labour' – men like printers, watchmakers, shipwrights and breeches-makers – characterised by their high wages, literacy and craft pride. Representing perhaps 10 per cent of the labour force in each trade, they enjoyed regular employment and felt entitled to regard themselves as men of consequence, with a claim to 'respectability'. Beneath them came the semi-skilled, an ill-defined group, with lower wages, less security and no traditions of apprenticeship. Factory operatives fell into this category. As a new social group, they attracted a great deal of attention from contemporary writers, and historians may have been misled by the weight of documentary evidence into over-estimating their importance. They were by no means typical of industrial workers in the middle years of the century, let alone of all workers. Of far greater consequence were the millions of domestic out-workers – hand-weavers, stocking knitters and nail-makers – who were

---

Source: Census of 1851, Ages and Occupations. After J. H. Clapham, *An Economic History of Modern Britain* (Cambridge University Press, 1932), vol. 2, p. 24.

Note: Agriculture and domestic service were still the greatest employers of labour as late as 1851 (partly because they were *per se* labour-intensive industries). Notice the large number of trades connected with clothing and transport services, and the dominance of women in certain occupations.

gradually succumbing to the challenge of mechanisation and being forced down into the ranks of the army of the unskilled. These unskilled workers comprised an immense variety of occupations – agricultural labourers, domestic servants, building workers, drovers and dockers, to name but some of the largest sub-categories. Poverty and illiteracy were the marks of their status, temporary or permanent indigence an accepted feature of their lives.

Social dislocation implies cultural dislocation, and the town worker failed to carry over ancient customs and pastimes, like rush bearing and cock fighting, into his new environment. It took longer for these features of traditional folk-lore to die out in the countryside, but in the 1870s the novelist Thomas Hardy was already complaining that music-hall jingles were driving out the old folk songs. The towns, newly created or transformed by industrialisation, scarcely looked capable of producing their own authentic cultural patterns. Many were abandoned by the middle classes who fled to new suburban villas in their search for better amenities and a diluted version of the life-style of the landed aristocrat. Greater physical distance implied greater social distance. As Canon Parkinson wrote of Manchester in 1841:

> The separation between the different classes, and the consequent ignorance of each others' habits and condition, are far more complete in this place than in any country of the older nations of Europe, or the agricultural parts of our own kingdom. There is far less personal communication between the master cotton spinner and his workmen, between the calico printer and his blue handed boys, than there is between the Duke of Wellington and the humblest labourer on his estate . . .

In the absence of middle-class leadership, urban workers were obliged to look to the apex of their own local hierarchy for appropriate values and life-styles. Consider, for instance, Disraeli's famous description of the social structure of fictional 'Wodgate', as portrayed in his novel, *Sybil*:

> These master workmen . . . form a powerful aristocracy, nor is it possible to conceive one apparently more oppressive. Their youths are worked for sixteen or even twenty hours a day; they are often sold by one master to another; they are fed on carrion and they sleep in lofts or cellars; yet whether it be that they are hardened by brutality, and really unconscious of their degrada-

tion and unusual sufferings, or whether they are supported by the belief that their day to be masters and oppressors will surely arrive, the aristocracy of Wodgate is by no means as unpopular as the aristocracy of most other places.

In the first place it is a real aristocracy; it is privileged, but it does something for its privileges. It is distinguished from the main body not merely by name. It is the most knowing class at Wodgate; it possesses indeed in its way complete knowledge; and it imparts in its manner a certain quantity of it to those whom it guides. Thus it is an aristocracy that leads, and therefore a fact. Moreover the social system of Wodgate is not an unvarying course of infinite toil. Their plan is to work hard, but not always. They seldom exceed four days of labour in the week. On Sunday the masters begin to drink; for the apprentices there is dog fighting without stint. On Monday and Tuesday the whole population of Wodgate is drunk. . . .

There are no others at Wodgate to preach or to control. . . . There are many in this town who are ignorant of their very names; very few who can spell them. It is rare that you meet with a young person who knows his own age; rarer to find the boy who has seen a book, or the girl who has seen a flower. Ask them the name of their sovereign, and they will give you an unmeaning stare; ask them the name of their religion, and they will laugh; who rules them on earth, or who can save them in Heaven, are alike mysteries to them.

Of course, Disraeli intended to shock his readers and painted his picture of urban society in the blackest colours, but it was from such unpromising material that a reasonably coherent and increasingly self-confident working class emerged by the end of the century. By 1900 the term 'working class' had lost its novelty and gained a new accuracy. The 'labouring classes' had become more homogeneous as mass-produced goods and a cheap popular press helped to eradicate regional differences in living. Mechanisation, moreover, enlarged the numbers and importance of semi-skilled 'machine minders' as a bridging group between the still powerful labour aristocrats and the rest of the labour force. The decline in the numbers employed in agriculture meant that the labour force became overwhelmingly industrial and urbanised. In these circumstances a new life-style and folk-culture came into being, particularly in the North and Midlands. Its distinctive features were (1) the extended family, centred around the mother or grandmother, which gave the individual the emotional support which circumstances had denied the first generation of town workers and which reaffirmed its solidarity in the rituals associated with birth, death and marriage; (2) the evolution of a new mass culture based on group activities like brass bands, choral societies and spectator pastimes like professional soccer and the music-hall; and (3) the reassertion of the old tradition of collectivism which had survived tenuously in the form of the Friendly Society and the 'funeral club' and now blossomed forth vigorously into militant industrial and political action.

The basic features of working-class existence had, however, remained unchanged. A small top layer could still aspire to middle-class status, while a rather larger bottom layer of paupers and vagrants reminded the mass of the penalties of failure in the 'opportunity' state. For most working men, mobility was limited by lack of access to appropriate education. Moreover, they were still a race apart, clearly defined by dress, speech and physique (in 1913 13-year-old boys at board school were on average five inches shorter than boys of the same age at public schools). They lived apart and still bore the stigma of manual labour, and, although the birth of a labour movement opened the eyes of a larger proportion of the working class than ever before to the possibilities of change through political and industrial action, there were still in 1914, as in 1845 when Disraeli coined the phrase, 'Two Nations'.

THE RISE OF THE MIDDLE CLASS

The middle class are always 'rising' and their 'rise' has been used to explain the Tudor despotism, the Civil War, inflation, enclosures and a dozen other historical phenomena. And yet the nineteenth century does see a transformation whereby the 'middling classes' of the pre-industrial world, became a self-conscious 'middle class'. Many historians seem to accept their self-image of themselves as heroic, industrious, liberal and religious. Less generous historians, usually of the Left, portray them as avaricious, philistine and hypocritical. They are the hero-villains of industrialisation and they stamped their values on the age they created.

Once again, close examination reveals the significant diversities within the great slab of society which began to call itself 'the middle class'. The upper echelons were filled by the great manufacturers, who had abandoned Nonconformism for the Established Church and forsaken the smoky scene of their entrepreneurial triumphs for a pastoral setting more in keeping with the social ambitions of their wives and the political ambitions of their sons. That acutely class-conscious novelist, Arnold Bennet, wrote of such men:

> Their assured, curt voices, their carriage, their clothes, the similarity of their manners, all show that they belong to a caste. . . . It has been called the middle class, but it ought to be called the upper class for nearly everything is below it. . . .

At the base of this particular pyramid were the publicans, small tradesmen and petty shopkeepers, who dealt in small quantities, handled the goods they sold and received payment in cash. Between these two strata the gulf was wide, but not so wide as the gulf that separated them from the lower orders who were unable to attain those badges of middle-class status – servants and a home of one's own.

It was the middle class which got the most benefits and suffered the least disruption from the process of industrialisation – a process which diversified it by producing wholly new professions and occupations such as engineers, managers, civil servants, etc. The Reform Act of 1832 admitted the middle class to political power, and the upper ranks of the bourgeoisie supplied such eminent statesmen as Peel and Gladstone. The middle-class life-style, with its emphasis on domestic propriety and religious observance, was widely adopted among the upper classes, at least in the middle decades of the century, and it was in these years that the assault on aristocratic privilege was strongest – the reforms of the 1830s being followed by the agitations of the Anti-Corn Law League and the outcry against aristocratic incompetence revealed in the Crimean War. The monumental institutional reforms of Gladstone's first Ministry (1868–74) which set the army, the judicial system and the civil service to rights, were the logical outcome of this pressure. Richard Cobden, the orator manufacturer, had delivered this warning to 'the high aristocracy of England' in the mid-1840s:

> . . . this is a new age; the age of social advancement . . . you belong to a mercantile age; you cannot have the advantage

of commercial rents and retain your feudal privileges, too. If you identify yourself with the spirit of the age, you may yet do well; for I tell you that the people of this country look to their aristocracy with a deep-rooted prejudice – an hereditary prejudice, I may call it – in their favour; but your power was never got, and you will not keep it by obstructing the progressive spirit of the age in which you live.

Cobden was right, and the aristocracy, as we shall see, knew it and acted accordingly.

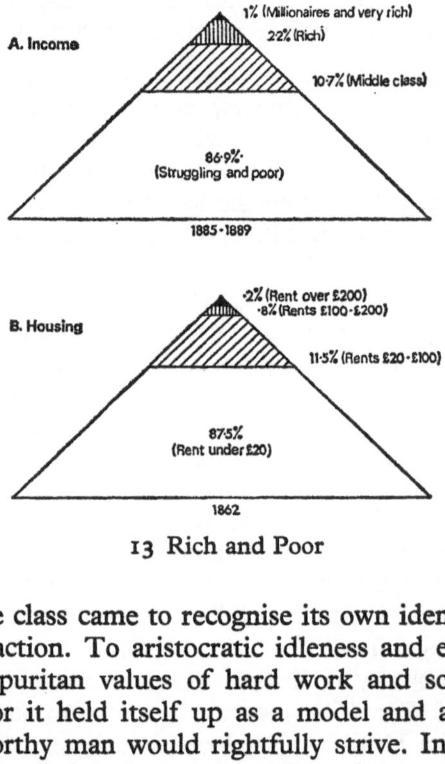

13 Rich and Poor

The middle class came to recognise its own identity through a process of reaction. To aristocratic idleness and extravagance it opposed the puritan values of hard work and sobriety, to the labouring poor it held itself up as a model and a goal towards which any worthy man would rightfully strive. Indeed, in some senses this was all that there was to give coherence to the middle classes. As John Burnett has put it:

Between the merchant and industrial princes and the petty bourgeoisie of tailors and milliners, chemists and elementary school teachers there was little in common except a dislike of those below and a distrust of those above them.

There were a number of more objective, if disputed, criteria for 'membership' of the middle class – an income of not less than £300 per annum, a certain degree of education, and familiarity with certain modes of social conduct. Internal dividing lines were also established – a home with proper servants' quarters, a private carriage, a connection with the aristocracy, or a son in a respected profession, were all marks of high social status within this heterogeneous, constantly growing group.

Broadly speaking, it may be said that in the first half of the nineteenth century the middle classes were concerned to establish their own identity, and so turn the profits of business into the basis of a distinctive way of life. This synthesis was achieved during the middle decades of the century and thereafter the middle class, while continuing to grow and diversify, lost some of its dynamism and self-assurance and concentrated instead on assimilating some of the aristocratic life-style of the disappearing pre-industrial world. Public schools and textbooks on etiquette were readily available to help them in their efforts, and the expansion of the Empire enabled their offspring to act like lords abroad, even if they could not do so at home.

THE SURVIVAL OF THE ARISTOCRACY

> In England an illustrious name is a great advantage and a cause of much pride to him who bears it, but in general one can say that the aristocracy is founded on wealth, a thing which may be *acquired*, and not on birth, which cannot. From this it results that one can clearly see in England where the aristocracy begins, but it is impossible to say where it ends. . . .
>
> The English aristocracy can therefore never arouse those violent hatreds felt by the middle and lower classes against the nobility of France where the nobility is an exclusive caste, which while monopolising all privileges and hurting everybody's feelings, offers no hope of ever entering into its ranks.
>
> The English aristocracy has a hand in everything: it is open to everyone: and anyone who wishes to abolish it or attack it as a body would have a hard task to define the object of his onslaught.

This analysis, by the perceptive de Tocqueville again, explains why the aristocracy survived the shocks and strains of the nineteenth century. It was not unwilling to recruit new members from below, and none of its characteristics could not be acquired, at least over a period of time. A coat of arms was long the mark of distinction, but the nineteenth century saw literally hundreds of new creations: in 1835 Baring, the financier, became Baron Ashburton; in 1856 Strutt, the industrialist, was likewise elevated to the House of Lords. In the 1880s, when agriculture was entering its deepest period of depression, the ranks of the armigerous were invaded by dozens eager to take up the financial strain of supporting a landed estate. Brassey, the son of the great contractor, became a peer in 1886, and the same decade saw so many brewing magnates ennobled – Guinness, Allsopp and Bass – that people began to refer jokingly to being elevated to 'the beerage'.

This rejuvenation-by-recruitment process, however, was largely an end-of-the-century phenomenon. The first phase of industrialisation had brought the aristocracy much wealth and little disruption of their traditional modes of life. Agriculture had prospered and rents risen at least until 1815, when the landed interest had been able to use its monopoly of Parliament to secure protection for corn growers. The practical failure of the corn laws served only to underline the advantages of diversifying one's source of income, and this the English aristocrat was well able to do. The convention that mineral wealth belonged, not to the Crown, as in most of Europe, but to the owner of the land under which it was found, made millionaires of the Marquis of Londonderry and the Earl of Durham. Urban developments made the fortunes of the Dukes of Bedford, Portland and Westmister, as the names of many streets and squares in London's West End will testify. Similarly, the Marquis of Bute turned some waste land into a priceless asset when Cardiff Docks were built upon it. Railway construction gave noble landowners the opportunity to milk the promoters of more than £100,000,000 for land sales and then plough it back into railway shares. And the desire of many new flotations to give an aristocratic lustre to their prospectus, made it easy for the less fortunate members of the élite to feather their nests by lending the name which was their only asset.

The fact that a name, a social asset as de Tocqueville observed in the passage quoted above, could be turned into hard cash, reveals a great deal about English society in the nineteenth century. Cobden, the self-styled spokesman of the self-righteous middle class, was disgusted by their fawning attitude towards their 'betters' – 'the insatiable love of caste, in England as in Hindustan, devours all hearts, is confined to no walks of society, but pervades every degree from the highest to the lowest'. The prevalence of this sentiment enabled the aristocracy to share their monopoly of political power without losing ultimate control. The Foreign Office, for instance, remained in aristocratic hands until the 1920s. Even the most aggressive bourgeois felt that such matters were the 'natural' concern of patricians. As Hippolyte Taine was informed by a prosperous manufacturer, '. . . we believe, we men of the middle class, that the conduct of national business calls for special men, men born and bred to the work for generations. . . .' In 1971, at the time of writing, these ancient prejudices still survive. The Exchequer, the Environment and Education are controlled by Ministers who have risen from the lower end of the middle class, but Defence, Foreign Affairs and the Law, the traditional and tradition-laden functions of the state, are still in the hands of a peer and two ex-peers.

FURTHER READING

J. Ryder and H. Silver, *Modern English Society – History and Structure, 1850–1970* (London, Methuen, 1971) is a good general account of social developments.

E. P. Thompson, *The Making of the English Working Class, 1780–1830* (Harmondsworth, Penguin, 1968) is the massive classic on the lower orders.

W. L. Guttsmann, *The British Political Élite* (London, MacGibbon, 1964) discusses the political power of the upper class.

Other useful works include:

G. D. H. Cole, *Studies in Class Structure* (London, Routledge, 1968).

Raymond Williams, *The Long Revolution* (Harmondsworth, Penguin, 1965).

Richard Hoggart, *The Uses of Literacy* (Harmondsworth, Penguin, 1969).

D. C. Marsh, *The Changing Social Structure of England and Wales, 1871–1961* (London, Routledge, 1965).

F. M. L. Thompson, *English Landed Society in the Nineteenth Century* (London, Routledge, 1963).

TABLE OF EVENTS

1776 Adam Smith's *Wealth of Nations*. American Declaration of Independence
1777
1778
1779 Iron bridge at Coalbrookdale
1780
1781
1782
1783 Britain recognises independence of U.S.A.
1784 Cort's puddling process. Watt patents rotary motion. First mail coaches
1785 Cartwright's first power loom
1786
1787 Grand Trunk Canal completed
1788
1789 French Revolution
1790
1791
1792
1793 Britain declares war on France. Cotton-gin invented in U.S.A.
1794
1795 Speenhamland System
1796
1797 Suspension of banknote convertibility
1798 T. R. Malthus's *Essay on Population*
1799 Passage of first Combination Laws. Income-tax introduced
1800 Union of Great Britain and Ireland
1801 First census. General Enclosure Act
1802 Peace of Amiens. Health and Morals of Apprentices Act
1803 War with France recommences. *Charlotte Dundas* (steamboat)
1804 Trevithick runs a locomotive at Pen-y-darryn colliery
1805
1806 Berlin Decree. Gas lighting of cotton mills
1807 Milan Decrees. Orders in Council. Abolition of slave trade in British Empire

1808
1809
1810
1811 Luddite activity at its peak
1812 Britain at war with United States (to 1814)
1813 East India Company loses monopoly of India trade
1814 Repeal of Statute of Artificers
1815 Peace with France. Corn Law. Davy's safety lamp
1816 Income-tax abolished
1817 March of the Blanketeers
1818
1819 Peterloo. Six Acts. *Savannah* crosses the Atlantic
1820
1821 Convertibility resumed. Gold standard introduced
1822 Power loom perfected. Cobbett's *Rural Rides*
1823 Huskisson begins tariff reforms (to 1827)
1824 Repeal of Combination Laws. Mechanics' Institute established in London
1825 Financial crisis. Stockton and Darlington Railway. Bubble Act repealed
1826 University of London founded
1827
1828 Sliding scale of corn duties. Neilson's hot air blast furnace
1829 Metropolitan Police established. Stephenson's *Rocket*
1830 Liverpool and Manchester Railway. Agricultural labourers revolt
1831 Cholera
1832 Great Reform Act
1833 Abolition of slavery. First effective Factory Act. First grant to education
1834 G.N.C.T.U. collapses. Poor Law Amendment Act. Tolpuddle Martyrs. Railway mania
1835 Municipal Reform Act
1836 Tithe Commutation Act. People's Charter drawn up. General Enclosure Act. Abolition of Tonnage Act
1837 Joint-stock organisation by letters patent. Registration of births, deaths and marriages. Construction of first railway telegraph
1838 Anti-Corn Law Association established in Manchester. Royal Agricultural Society established
1839 Severe depression (to 1842)
1840 Penny post. Nasmyth's steam-hammer
1841 Fall of Whig government
1842 Peel's Free Trade budgets begin (to 1845). Mines and Collieries Act. Establishment of Rothamsted Experimental Station
1843 Income-tax re-introduced
1844 Bank Charter Act. Rochdale Pioneers begin first Co-op

1845 Irish famine. First agricultural college opened at Cirencester. General Enclosure Act
1846 Repeal of the Corn Laws
1847 Commercial crisis. Bank Charter Act suspended. Ten Hours Act
1848 Great Chartist demonstration. General Board of Health established. Public Health Act
1849 Repeal of Navigation Laws
1850
1851 Great Exhibition. Engineers' New Model union. Channel cable laid
1852
1853
1854 Crimean War (to 1856)
1855 Paris Universal Exhibition
1856 Bessemer converter. First aniline dye discovered
1857 Indian Mutiny. Commercial crisis. Second suspension of Bank Charter Act
1858
1859
1860 Cobden–Chevalier trade treaty
1861 American Civil War begins (to 1865). Post Office Savings Bank established
1862 Legislation on limited liability consolidated
1863 Co-operative Wholesale Society
1864 Siemens–Martin open-hearth furnace
1864 'Red Flag Act'
1866 Overend-Gurney crisis. Third suspension of Bank Act. Atlantic cable laid. 'Sheffield Outrages'
1867 Second Reform Act gives vote to urban workers. Royal Commission on Trade Unions. Hornby *v.* Close
1868 T.U.C. meets for first time
1869 Suez Canal opened. Torrens Act
1870 Elementary Education Act passed
1871 Trade Union Act. Local Government Board
1872 Secret Ballot. First agricultural workers unions
1873 End of the last great boom – beginning of 'Great Depression' (to 1896)
1874
1875 Disraeli buys Suez Canal shares. 'Plimsoll' Act. Public Health Act. Cross Act. Conspiracy and Protection of Property Act. Gilchrist-Thomas basic steel process
1876
1877
1878
1879

1880 Salvation Army. Frozen meat imported from Australia
1881
1882
1883 Fabian Society founded
1884 Franchise granted to rural workers. Reform Act
1885 Royal Commission on Housing. Rover 'safety bicycle'
1886 Unemployed riot in Trafalgar Square
1887
1888 County Councils established. 'Fair Trade' agitation. Pneumatic tyre
1889 London Dock Strike. Technical Education Act
1890 Baring crisis. Housing Act. First electric tube railway
1891 Free elementary education
1892
1893
1894
1895
1896 Repealed Red Flag Act
1897 Workmen's compensation improved
1898 Imperial penny postage
1899 Boer War (to 1902)
1900
1901 Taff Vale judgement
1902 Local education authorities established. Certification of Midwives
1903 Tariff Reform League established
1904
1905 Liberal government elected
1906 Trade Union Act reverses Taff Vale judgement. School meals for poor children
1907 First census of production. School medical inspections
1908 Coal Mines Regulations Act. Old-Age Pension Scheme introduced
1909 Lloyd George's 'People's Budget'. Labour Exchanges. Trade Boards Act. Town and County Planning Act. Report of the Royal Commission on the Poor Law and Unemployment
1910
1911 Health and unemployment insurance. National transport strikes
1912 Shops Act
1913
1914 Triple Alliance. Outbreak of Great War

Index of Names